TARGET
Reading Accuracy

TARGET
Reading Accuracy

Essential Reading for Effective Learning

For Class Teachers, SENCOs, Classroom Assistants and Support for Learning Staff

Bernadette McLean
and Rosie Wood

Barrington Stoke
Helen Arkell Dyslexia Centre

First published 2004 in Great Britain by Barrington Stoke Ltd,
Sandeman House, Trunk's Close, 55 High Street, Edinburgh, EH1 1SR

www.barringtonstoke.co.uk

Copyright © 2004 Helen Arkell Dyslexia Centre

ISBN 1-84299-156-6

Editor: Julia Rowlandson

Original cover idea by Stuart Boyde

Designed and typeset by GreenGate Publishing Services, Tonbridge
Printed in China by Sino Publishing House Ltd

Contents

For simplicity, in this book the student will be referred to as 'he' and the teacher as 'she'.

Introduction

Target Reading Accuracy is a practical tool for teachers and classroom assistants to enable them to guide readers towards accurate and rapid word recognition. This leaves mental energy for thinking about and understanding the content of what they read. It is the precursor to *Target Reading Comprehension*, the companion volume offering practical tips and activities to develop effective reading comprehension.

Activities are suitable for struggling readers at upper primary and secondary levels.

What you will find in this book

- **A system** to enable readers to read more accurately and fluently.

- **Assessment** to determine breakdown points in reading accuracy and where to begin with remediation.

- **A guide for teachers** and classroom assistants at the end of this chapter to find the appropriate sections in this book, and in *Target Reading Comprehension*, to provide the necessary support.

- **A checklist for the teacher** to use whilst the pupil is reading.

- **A checklist (photocopiable) for the reader** to use with teacher support to pinpoint his reading difficulties, see Chapter 8. He will become more motivated if he plays a part in devising his own targets.

- **Individualised teaching points** in the form of a skill building programme with teaching ideas and ways to encourage accurate reading.

- **Photocopiable sheets** which provide activities to be used with individuals or groups.

- **A structured approach** including accurate and fluent decoding, other ways of reading words on sight, the visual skills which are necessary and issues of readability.

- **Target cards** which prompt activities for readers to carry out independently or with the support of a helper.

What reading is:

- Effective readers read with accuracy, at a reasonable speed, understand what they are reading and recall the read material once the reading activity is over.

- Effective readers use 'bottom-up' strategies to support reading and 'top-down' strategies to monitor and check accuracy and understanding.

> **Bottom-up** starts with learning about letter/sound links and using phonics. This is the approach used in *Target Reading Accuracy*.
>
> **Top-down** uses knowledge of grammar and meaning to help predict words. This is the approach used in *Target Reading Comprehension*.

- Reading is a learned skill that needs to be taught: *'Reading is not a natural activity, but a set of gradually acquired component skills learned independently, but later integrated and automated .... There is no single straight path to competence in reading. ...'* (Turner, 1995)[1]

See Appendix I on page 111 for 'Normal development of reading'.

See Appendix II on page 114 for 'Reading tests'.

---

1   Turner, M. (1995) 'Children learn to read by being taught', in Owen, P. and Pumfrey, P.D. (eds) *Children Learning to Read*, Vol. 1. London: Falmer Press.

What you need for reading

- Good eyesight and good hearing which lead to good visual processing and the ability to learn about sounds in words.

- Experience and knowledge of the world.

- Good language skills:
  - a wide vocabulary
  - mastery of grammatical constructions in spoken language
  - good understanding of spoken language.

- Awareness of concepts of print:
  - directionality of words from left to right and moving from one line to the next
  - orientation of letters which are easily confused, e.g. *b/d, u/n, m/w, t/f, p/q*
  - the same letter in different forms, e.g. a, A, a, **A**
  - sequence of letters and words, e.g. *on/no, saw/was.*
    The dog bit the man. / The man bit the dog.
  - letter/sound links, e.g. *c = /k/ or /s/,*
    ea as in *seat, break, bread.*

Pages 6–10 are a guide for teachers and classroom assistants on where to start with reading remediation. Use this with the photocopiable checklist on page 11 which is for teachers and support assistants to use while listening to students reading.

Select a sufficiently challenging text, i.e. 90–95% words are easy to read. If the text is too easy, difficulties will not become apparent. If it is too difficult, the reader will become frustrated and have a poor understanding of what he is reading.

Fill in this checklist as you listen to the student read.

20 Questions

Guide for teachers and classroom assistants on where to start with reading remediation

Listen to the reader reading text at a sufficiently challenging level, i.e. 90–95% of words are easy to read. If the text is too easy to read, difficulties will not be apparent. If it is too difficult, it will be at frustration level and the reader will have poor understanding of what he is reading.

The following is a guide to help you to fill in the checklist (page 11) and to decide where to begin with remediation. References are to this book (TRA) and *TRC, Target Reading Comprehension*.

Questions to ask	Think about …	Action to take	References
1 Is he reluctant to tackle reading tasks?	This may be because he lacks confidence because he has failed in the past.	Check reading level of text. If it is too hard, try easier text. See Chapter 6. Check knowledge of high frequency words.	Ch. 6 TRA 'Readability' Ch. 4 TRA 'Word Reading'
2 Is he willing to try if he does not know a word?	If not, he may be lacking in confidence as above, or he may still be at an early reading development stage.	Build phonological awareness and word attack strategies.	Ch. 3 TRA 'Phonological Awareness and Phonics' Ch. 4 TRA 'Word Reading'
3 Does he use the letters in the word to help sound out an unfamiliar word?	If not, he may not be linking the letter strings with sounds.	Teach phonological awareness and decoding.	Ch. 3 TRA 'Phonological Awareness and Phonics'

Cont'd

	Questions to ask	Think about …	Action to take	References
4	Does he have difficulty with longer words?	He may not have word attack skills due to difficulties with phonological awareness or a lack of understanding of the structure of words, e.g. *revisiting* where *re* is the prefix, *visit* is the root word and *ing* is the suffix.	Build phonological awareness and teach the structure of words, e.g. prefixes, root words, suffixes.	Ch. 3 TRA 'Phonological Awareness and Phonics' Ch. 4 TRA 'Word Reading' *Ch. 3 TRC 'Word Reading – Vocabulary Extension'*
5	Does he lack fluency when he reads?	He may be having to work out or sound out too many words.	Build up automaticity at word level, beginning with high frequency words.	Ch. 4 TRA 'Word Reading'
6	Are his substitutions not real words?	There may be an underlying spoken language difficulty. He may have a poor vocabulary.	Develop a larger and more flexible vocabulary.	*Ch. 3 TRC 'Word Reading – Vocabulary Extension'*
7	Do real word substitutions make sense in the context?	He may be over-reliant on the context at the expense of accurate decoding.	Develop decoding skills.	Ch. 3 TRA 'Phonological Awareness and Phonics'
8	Do real word substitutions **not** make sense in the context?	He may not be monitoring the sense of the word within the whole sentence.	Teach whole sentence comprehension.	*Ch. 4 TRC 'Sentences'*
9	Does he rarely or never self-correct?	He may not be monitoring his comprehension as he reads.	Help him to develop ways of monitoring his understanding while he is reading.	*Ch. 8 TRC 'Interactive Reading'*

Cont'd

Questions to ask	Think about ...	Action to take	References
10 What use does he make of pictorial or other visual clues in the text?	1 If he does not use them he may have visual processing problems. 2 If he is over-reliant on visual information it may indicate a lack of reading fluency or the level of text is too difficult.	1 Check visual processing and consider referral. 2 Build up automaticity at word level beginning with high frequency words. Check level of text.	Ch. 5 TRA 'Visual Processing' Ch. 4 TRA 'Word Reading' Ch. 6 TRA 'Readability'
11 Does he read word by word without grouping words into phrases?	He may lack sufficient fluency in reading words and phrases.	Build automaticity at word level. Build phrase-reading ability.	Ch. 4 TRA 'Word Reading' *Ch. 4 TRC 'Sentences'*
12 Does he repeat words and/or phrases?	This may indicate: 1 a memory problem or 2 a visual scanning problem.	1 Teach visualisation skills. 2 Check visual processing and consider referral.	*Ch. 9 TRC 'Visualisation'* Ch. 5 TRA 'Visual Processing'
13 Does he have difficulty with left to right scanning and keeping his place? Does he hold the book at an unusual angle or very close to his eyes? Does he screw up his eyes? Does he finger point? Does he leave out or add little words?	Any or all of these may indicate visual processing problems.	Check visual processing and refer for optometric assessment.	Ch. 5 TRA 'Visual Processing'

Cont'd

Questions to ask	Think about ...	Action to take	References
14 Does he notice punctuation?	If not, this may indicate: 1 a visual processing problem 2 a comprehension problem because he is not attending to phrase and sentence boundaries.	1 Check visual processing. 2 Develop comprehension skills starting at sentence level and moving to longer pieces of text.	1 Ch. 5 TRA 'Visual Processing' 2 Ch. 4 TRC 'Sentences' Ch. 5 TRC 'Paragrpahs and Longer Texts'
15 Does he read too quickly?	He may be a skimmer, not attending to detail in the text.	Teach him how to notice detail in the text.	Ch. 4 TRA 'Word Reading' (Bingo lookalike words and Snap) Ch. 3 TRC 'Sentences' (Order of words, Yes/No/Maybe and Same or Different)
16 Does he read too slowly?	1 He may be a plodder, working out the majority of words because he is unable to read words at sight. 2 He does not know when or how to skim read. 3 He may be focusing on decoding skills at the expense of comprehension.	1 Build automaticity at word level beginning with high frequency words. 2 Teach reading strategies to suit purposes of reading. 3 Teach comprehension skills starting at sentence level.	1 Ch. 4 TRA 'Word Reading' 2 Ch. 7 TRC 'Types of Reading' 3 Ch. 4 TRC 'Sentences' Ch. 5 TRC 'Paragraphs and Longer Texts'
17 Does he read accurately but with little comprehension or recall of the text once the reading activity is over?	He may be a passive reader who is not interacting with the text.	Teach ways of interacting with text and how to visualise.	Ch. 8 TRC 'Interactive Reading' Ch. 9 TRC 'Visualisation'

Cont'd

Questions to ask	Think about ...	Action to take	References
18 Does he find the vocabulary or the concepts too difficult?	**1** He may not know the words. **2** He may lack familiarity with the topic.	**1** Help extend his vocabulary. **2** Build familiarity with the topic before reading. **3** Teach KWL and SKWL.	**1** *Ch. 3 TRC 'Word Reading'* **2** *Ch. 6 TRC 'Listening to Reading'* **3** *Ch. 8 TRC 'Interactive Reading' (KWL and SKWL)*
19 Does he read all texts in the same way?	He may lack the necessary flexibility to adjust his approach dependent on the reason for reading.	Teach different strategies for reading and when to use them.	*Ch. 7 TRC 'Types of Reading'*
20 Does he enjoy reading?	If not, he may be reading books that are too easy or too difficult.	Check reading level. Teach him how to choose the right level.	*Ch. 6 TRA 'Readability'* *Ch. 6 TRC 'Listening to Reading'*

20 QUESTIONS CHECKLIST

20 questions to ask:	Yes/No	Comments:
1 Is he reluctant to tackle reading tasks?		
2 Is he willing to try if he does not know a word?		
3 Does he use the letters in the word to help sound out an unfamiliar word?		
4 Does he have difficulty with longer words?		
5 Does he lack fluency when he reads?		
6 Are his substitutions not real words?		
7 Do real word substitutions make sense in the context?		
8 Do real word substitutions **not** make sense in the context?		
9 Does he rarely or never self-correct?		
10 Does he use pictorial or other visual clues in the text?		
11 Does he read word by word without grouping words into phrases?		
12 Does he repeat words and/or phrases?		
13 Does he have difficulty with left to right scanning and keeping his place? Does he hold the book at an unusual angle or very close to his eyes? Does he screw up his eyes? Does he finger point? Does he leave out or add little words?		
14 Does he notice punctuation?		
15 Does he read too quickly?		
16 Does he read too slowly?		
17 Does he read accurately but with little comprehension or recall of the text once the reading activity is over?		
18 Does he find the vocabulary or the concepts too difficult?		
19 Does he read all texts in the same way?		
20 Does he not enjoy reading?		

Introduction to Decoding

Decoding is the process of deciphering the written letters on the page and turning them into words that can be spoken. Decoding enables the reader to do this even if he does not understand the word. For instance, it is the way competent readers read a nonsense word (such as *strell*) or a new place name (such as *Plemington*).

Phonics teaching trains readers to make the translation from written letters to spoken words.

The teaching of literacy in the English language has to involve phonics because English is an alphabetic script, i.e. the letters used to spell words on the page are closely related to the sounds of those spoken words. The beginning reader decodes the sequence of letters in order to retrieve the sound pattern of a word. From the sound pattern he can move to the meaning.

There are three types of spelling for words in English:

1. **Absolutely regular**, e.g. *hot, crab, step, lump*.
   In these words each sound has a corresponding letter or letters. The word can be sounded out letter by letter.

2. **Rule based**, e.g. *came, stiff, swimmer*.
   These are sound based, phonic rules which determine the spelling pattern.
   - In *came* the silent *e* at the end makes the *a* have its long sound.
   - In *stiff* the double *ff* comes after a short vowel sound.
   - In *swimmer* the double *mm* comes after a short vowel before a suffix beginning with a vowel.

3   **Irregular**, e.g. *said, yacht, because.*

- The letter pattern is not so closely linked to the sound order but still gives clues to the pronunciation, e.g. <u>sai</u>d <u>y</u>ach<u>t</u> <u>bec</u>au<u>s</u>e.

In order to decode and read words accurately the reader needs to:

- be aware of, and reflect on, the sound stream of words – **phonological awareness**
- know the precise links between sounds and written letters – **sound/letter links**
- know the **phonic rules** such as silent *e* and double letters
- recognise **frequent letter patterns**, such as *ed, ing, tion.*

Of course, once words are 'known' they are recognised and read automatically, but all readers have to go back to decoding for unfamiliar words such as place names.

Consider reading *'Splagthrish'* or *'Dultinghame'.*

In sounding out a word the reader:

- converts the letter string into sounds
- blends these sounds together
- adds any knowledge of phonic patterns
- pronounces the word.

When children come to school they move from 'learning to talk' to 'talking to learn', and in order to learn to read and spell they need to recognise that the sounds of speech are related to the letters on the page. Phonological awareness and the accompanying skills described above are the necessary links.

Many students are lucky and phonological awareness seems to develop spontaneously; others will need explicit teaching. For this, see Chapter 3 – 'Phonological Awareness and Phonics'.

Phonological Awareness and Phonics

Phonics is based on the sounds in words. Therefore phonological awareness is an essential underpinning set of skills in order to be able to understand and use phonic rules. Teaching phonics to those who lack this essential underpinning knowledge is a waste of valuable time.

Before beginning to teach phonics, check that students have competent phonological awareness.

Phonological awareness can be described in terms of a hierarchy of individual skills with **spoken** words.

The following are all **listening** skills:

A Auditory discrimination

Is the student able to distinguish between words in which there are similar sounds?

> e.g.   *some/sun*   *though/foe*

B Segmentation skills

Can the student use all *three* ways of breaking up the sound stream of a spoken word: syllables, onset and rime and phonemes?

Syllables

Can the student hear the 'beats' in a word and recognise that there is a vowel sound in each one?

> e.g.   hel..i..cop..ter   hol..i..day   su..per..mar..ket
> re..cor..ding

Onset and rime

Can the student divide a single syllable word?

> e.g.   d..og   st..op   w..atch   ch..ips   cr..oss   str..ing

or a syllable within a word,

> e.g.   pl..at/f..orm   ch..ap/t..er

into the consonant sound(s) at the beginning of the syllable (onset) and the vowel sound onwards (rime).

NB Sometimes, a syllable consists of a rime only,

> e.g.   and   ex..pl..ain (the first syllable)
> h..ol..i..d..ay (the middle syllable)

> **Onset** – the initial consonant(s) in a word or syllable.
>
> **Rime** – the vowel and any letters after it in a syllable.

Phonemes

Can the student divide words into the smallest units of sound (phonemes) which can signify a difference in meaning, such as **bean / mean, tab / dab**?

> **Phoneme** – the smallest unit of sound in a word.

> e.g.   s..t..r..aw   ch..a..p..t..er   c..r..o..ss   s..t..r..i..ng

The ability to blend and to segment these component segments of sounds underpins the phonic skills for reading and spelling.

C Rhyme and alliteration

Is the student aware of **rhyme** and **alliteration**?

> **Alliteration** – words which start with the same sound, e.g. <u>H</u>orrid <u>H</u>enry <u>h</u>ates <u>h</u>amsters.
>
> Note that the sound does not always correspond with the same letters, e.g. *car, choir, kind*.

Rhyme

e.g. *cat/hat   string/thing   table/fable
cooking/looking*

Alliteration

e.g. *mouse, Mary, mine, more, move
chips, cheese, chives
place, please, plant*

The ability to detect and generate rhyme and alliteration helps an individual to decode. Alliteration gives the all-important first sound as a clue. Rhyme helps to form analogies between sound patterns and written patterns in words, where the sound and letter patterns match.

e.g. *s..ock r..ock fl..ock,
r..ain m..ain pl..ain*

D Letter/sound links

Can the student make automatic links between the letters on the page and their sounds? This is essential for fluent decoding.

In English there are 26 letters for at least 44 phonemes. There is a certain amount of overlap.

Some sounds are represented by more than one letter, e.g. the sound **/oh/** might be written as th**ough**, rainb**ow**, **o**ver, h**oe**, etc.

Some letters represent more than one sound, e.g. the letter **c** may be sounded differently as in **c**ertain, **c**hop, **c**at.

Variations can be learnt after learning the most common correspondences between letters and sounds.

When you say the individual sounds it is important to keep the sound as pure as possible. If the schwa vowel (an /uh/ sound) is added, this can distort the blending process.

> e.g. in blending the sounds for sat, /suh/+/a/+/tuh/ makes **suhatuh**
>
> but blending the sounds without the schwa vowel, /s/ + /a/ + /t/, makes **sat**.

---

schwa vowel = an /uh/ sound.

When beginning readers learn letter/sound links, it is important that they learn each sound as purely as possible. They should say a word and listen to the individual letter sounds.

For correct letter/sound links see Sheet 3.1 – 'Correct Sounds for Letters'.

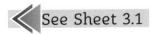 See Sheet 3.1

A natural development or taught skills?

Many students will become aware of rhymes and alliteration quite naturally. They may also divide words into syllables spontaneously. Some will make analogies between rimes and letter groups with ease. The ability to link sounds and letter groups becomes increasingly refined and detailed. Students will also become familiar with regular letter strings such as **ing**, **tion** and **ed**.

If this awareness does not develop, it will need explicit teaching. Many students will need guidance and teaching for phoneme awareness, i.e. the ability to segment words into their smallest sounds.

ASSESSMENT

A simple screening device is to ask students to read absolutely regular non-words, such as *spleg, fontosh*.

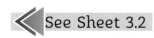 See Sheet 3.2

If students are able to read these words accurately, it is likely that they have sufficiently well developed phonological awareness and letter/sound links for decoding.

More detailed assessment should include listening activities:

- Auditory discrimination (e.g. *ton/done*) Are these two words the same or different? If auditory discrimination is very weak, refer for a hearing test.

- Segmentation and blending at the levels of:
  - syllable, e.g. *ad – vert – ise – ment*
  - onset and rime, e.g. *c – ook*
  - phoneme, e.g. *c – r – a – sh*
    (**NB** alliteration often comes before appreciation of later phonemes in a word. It is easier to segment the first sound of a word than sounds which come later.)
  - rhyme judgement, e.g. do *thing* and *ring* rhyme?
  - rhyme production, e.g. Say as many words as you can which rhyme with *flap*.

> When assessing phonological awareness, do not let students see the written words. These are **listening** activities.

There are many phonological awareness assessments now available, most of which are administered on an individual basis. Those suitable for upper primary and secondary students include the ones shown on the following page.

Phonological awareness assessments

Helen Arkell Dyslexia Centre Auditory Tests – Revised Version 2000
Helen Arkell Dyslexia Centre, Frensham, Farnham, Surrey GU10 3BW, Tel: 01252 797511

Phonological Assessment Battery (PhAB) by Norah Frederickson, Uta Frith and Rea Reason
NFER-NELSON Publishing Co Ltd, The Chiswick Centre, 414 Chiswick High Road, London W4 5TF, Tel: 0845 6021937

Sound Linkage by Peter Hatcher
Whurr Publishers, Turpin Distribution Services Ltd, Blackhorse Road, Letchworth, Hertfordshire SG6 1HN, Tel: 01462 672555

ACTIVITIES

There are many activities and games to promote phonological awareness and letter/sound links, which are suitable for group work.

- Adapt commercial games or create home-made games to practise each skill.
- Make games of Snap, Pairs or Happy Families using small cards.
- Make simple Bingo and race games from larger pieces of card.

When making or adapting games, be careful to think about the aim of the exercise. Ask the following:

- Is the activity to *detect* or *produce* the skill (e.g. rhyme)?
- How long is it likely to take?
- Does it place an unnecessary load on memory?
- Will the pupil sound out aloud?
- Are the pictures/words likely to be familiar?
- How many people can play the game together?
- Have you tried the game? Does it work?
- Are *pictures*, *written* words or both to be used?
- Have you provided clear instructions?
- If written words are used, are letter patterns the same? (*hot/pot/yacht*)
- Would non-words help the student focus on the phonological skills better?
- If non-words are used, are they absolutely regular? (*Splag* is regular, but *pleme* requires knowledge of silent *e* rule.)

Auditory discrimination

Short but regular training activities can help discrimination.

- Start with obvious differences and move towards more subtle ones.
- Use hands on resources.
- Use visual support.
- Increase difficulty level gradually.

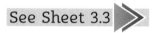

For a guide to auditory discrimination training, see Sheet 3.3 – 'Auditory Discrimination'.

Minimal pairs can form useful practice, e.g. *tip/dip, tank/dank, tell/dell*.

> **Minimal pairs** are pairs of words in which the difference in meaning is signalled by one sound only.

NB Do not show the student the written words when practising this activity.

Syllable division

Some students will benefit from using touch and movement to help them listen.

Encourage students to:

- move arms or hands in time to syllable beats in words
- place fingers under the jaw when saying polysyllabic words; this will enable the student to feel the downward movement with each vowel sound
- clap hands for each syllable
- count the syllables
- tap fingers or place counters for each syllable.

NB Use polysyllabic words in games and activities where syllables have to be counted.

Pairs game

- Make two sets of cards with pictures on one set and corresponding words on the second set.
- Write the number of syllables on the back of each word card.
- Each player picks up a picture card first, says the word, counts the syllables and then picks up a word card with the correct number of syllables on the back.

  NB. Help may be needed at this reading stage.
- If the picture and word match, the player claims the pair.
- If the cards do not match, they are placed face down again.
- The winner is the player with most pairs at the end.

Talking turns

- Ask students to say the syllables of words, phrases or sentences alternately with another person.
- Use words with which they are familiar, such as the names of footballers, pop stars, television programmes, etc.
- Where possible, use words and phrases in which the individual syllables can be easily separated.
- For a list of suitable words, see Sheet 3.4 – 'Syllable Division'.

  NB Do not let students see the written words as this is a listening, not a reading activity.

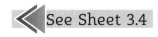
See Sheet 3.4

For further syllable activities see Target Cards 3.1, 3.2 and 3.3.

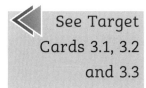
See Target Cards 3.1, 3.2 and 3.3

Rhyme judgement and production

- Practise rhyme skills with games. There are some commercial games available such as rhyming Snap.

- Use appealing books, written in rhyme, such as Roald Dahl's *Revolting Rhymes*. Ask the student to say the rhyming word:

  e.g. *The Ugly Sisters, jewels and* **all,**
  Departed for the Palace ... **Ball.**

- Ask students to make up rhyming couplets:

  e.g. *We went in the* **car**
  But we didn't go ... **far.**

- Give activities in which students listen for the odd one out in a group of rhyming words,

  e.g. *book   look   **tank**   cook.*

  Follow this by asking the student to give an additional rhyming word for the list, e.g. *took.*

- Play games such as Bingo where students collect words (of similar written patterns) to match a target word. This will promote the links between the sound and letter patterns.

  e.g. *wing* ... *thing* ... *bring* ... *fling* ... *king* ...
  to match a picture Bingo card of a ring.

- Encourage internal rhyming ability by asking students to do some activities without saying the words aloud. Do this once they can manage rhyming tasks which include listening and speaking aloud.

See Target Card 3.4

For a further rhyming activity see Target Card 3.4.

24

Onset and rime

- Ask students to put onsets and rimes together and to say the whole word aloud. Use both real and non-words e.g. *st..op* and *st..ap*. This encourages the phonological awareness of these segments in words and links them to the written letters. Make sure the segments are visually clear by writing them on cards, using the Edith Norrie Letter Case or plastic letters.

In the Edith Norrie Letter Case the letters are placed in the box according to where the sound is made in the mouth. This adds tactile information to support the weak auditory skill.

The Edith Norrie Letter Case is obtainable from the Helen Arkell Dyslexia Centre, Frensham, Farnham, Surrey GU10 3BW, Tel: 01252 79 7511

- Keep the segments simple at the beginning.
- Later, add letters which have different sounds, such as soft *c/g* or *w*. 'W' changes the following 'a' to sound like /ŏ/ (e.g. *sash, cash, wash*).
  Add phonic families, such as *... ice ... all ... ame*.

Onset and rime card game

- Write onsets on cards in one colour and rimes on cards in a second colour.
- Place the cards in two piles.
- Each player starts with three onset cards.
- Turn up one rime card.
- The first player sounds out the options available to him with his rimes, moving the rime alongside his onset cards in order to 'read' the words or non-words which are formed.
- When a real word is made, it is claimed and put aside, and another onset card is added to make the third.
- Players take turns and the winner is the one with the most real words at the end.

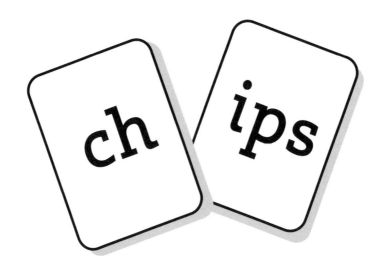

See Sheet 3.5 ▶ For onsets and rimes which are suitable for games, see Sheet 3.5 – 'Onsets and Rimes'.

Rabbit

Tiger

Tie.

Alliteration

- Teach alliteration.

- Play 'Silly I Spy'; this helps students to understand the principle of alliteration. Say a word in which the first sound is changed, e.g. I spy a **vettle**. The players have to guess the word – a **kettle**.

- Once the principle of alliteration is understood, ask students to:
  - sort picture cards into first sound groups (which can be checked by having the written words on the back)
  - play odd one out activities, e.g. say a list of words or present a group of pictures in which one is the odd man out because it does not have the same first sound
  - play games, e.g. 'I went to market ...', where each item has to begin with the same sound.

- If a student has real difficulty segmenting the first sounds of words, start with these sounds, which can easily be elongated:
  f / m / n / s / v / z

26

- Use a drill to learn letter/sound links.
  - Make picture cards for the alphabet with the picture on one side and the letter on the reverse.
  - Ask the student to look at the **letter** first, say the **whole word** by recalling the picture on the other side and then say the **first sound**.
  - Go through the whole pack of cards as a drill.
  - Repeat frequently and use a timer to encourage the student to speed up.
  - Get the student to practise until the whole activity is automatic.

> **Automaticity** – when a skill becomes spontaneous and effortless.

For further alliteration activities, see Target Cards 3.5, 3.6 and 3.7.

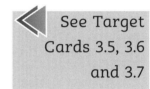

See Target Cards 3.5, 3.6 and 3.7

Phoneme segmentation and blending

When teaching phoneme segmentation and blending:

- Use absolutely regular words, i.e. those words which can be sounded out letter by letter, e.g. *stop, cramp, frog*.

- Give visual and tactile support:
  - Use coloured counters to represent the sounds of a spoken word,
    e.g. *s p o t* as
    Say *spot*.

  - Ask the student to take away the right counter when one sound is removed,
    e.g. Say *p o t*.
    Student removes the first counter.

27

- Ask the student to change the counter if a sound is changed,

  e.g. Say *p e t*.

- Remember students can become confused when they try to listen for phonemes in real words as they may already have some idea of how the word is written and may recall this visual image rather than listening to the actual sound sequence. It can help to use absolutely regular non-words. Start with a simple sound sequence and gradually add more complex ones as follows:
  - non-words of three phonemes, e.g. *gat*
  - consonant blends (or digraphs) at the beginning, e.g. **sn**at (**th**ap)
  - consonant blends (or digraphs) at the end, e.g. di**st** (di**th**)
  - two syllables, e.g. *flotpem*.

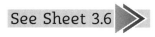

For non-words graded in difficulty, see Sheet 3.6 – 'Non-words'.

- Use these non-words in activities for encoding (spelling) and decoding (reading). This will give the student experience in turning sound sequences into letter sequences and vice versa.

- Devise games in which students work in pairs to read out non-words for the other to spell, using plastic letters or the Edith Norrie Letter Case. Commercial board games can be adapted.

- **Word chains** are an excellent way to support phoneme awareness, e.g.

  twig ... twit ... twist ... twin ... win ... wins ... wink.

  Use one-syllable, absolutely regular words from Sheet 3.7 – 'Word Chains'.

  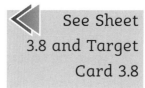
  See Sheet 3.7

  - Ask the student to make the first word with letters from the Edith Norrie Letter Case or plastic letters.
  - Tell the student to listen carefully to the order of sounds and therefore letters.
  - Say the next word.
  - Ask him to listen to where the difference in sound occurs.
  - Ask him to identify where the sound pattern has changed and to change the corresponding letter or letters.
  - Say the next word and repeat as above.

- Play games in which the student has to say words again leaving out a sound, e.g. say *snap* without the /s/.

This activity of taking away a phoneme to make a second word (or non-word) helps students who are sometimes unsure how many sounds there are in consonant blends.

See Sheet 3.8 – 'Phoneme Deletion' and Target Card 3.8.

See Sheet 3.8 and Target Card 3.8

Correct Sounds for Letters

These are the correct common sounds for each letter of the alphabet. Be careful to pronounce them without an added schwa vowel (an /uh/ sound).

a   as in apple
b   as in ball
c   as in cat (/k/ not kuh)
d   as in dog
e   as in egg
f   as in four (/fff/ not fuh)
g   as in garden
h   as in house (/h/ not huh)
i   as in igloo
j   as in jar
k   as in king (/k/ not kuh)
l   as in leg (/l/ not luh)
m   as in man (/mmm/ not muh)
n   as in nut (/nnn/ not nuh)
o   as in orange
p   as in pie (/p/ not puh)
q   as in queen
r   as in robin
s   as in sun (/sss/ not suh)
t   as in tie (/t/ not tuh)
u   as in umbrella
v   as in violin (/vvv/ not vuh)
w   as in water
x   as in fox (/ks/ not eks)
y   as in yacht
z   as in zebra (/zzz/ not zuh)

NB Repetition of the letter to give the correct sound means lengthening it slightly, **not** repeating the sound.

Non-word Screening Test

The following non-words are a useful screening test for phonological awareness. Ask the student to 'read' the words. Write down what the student says.

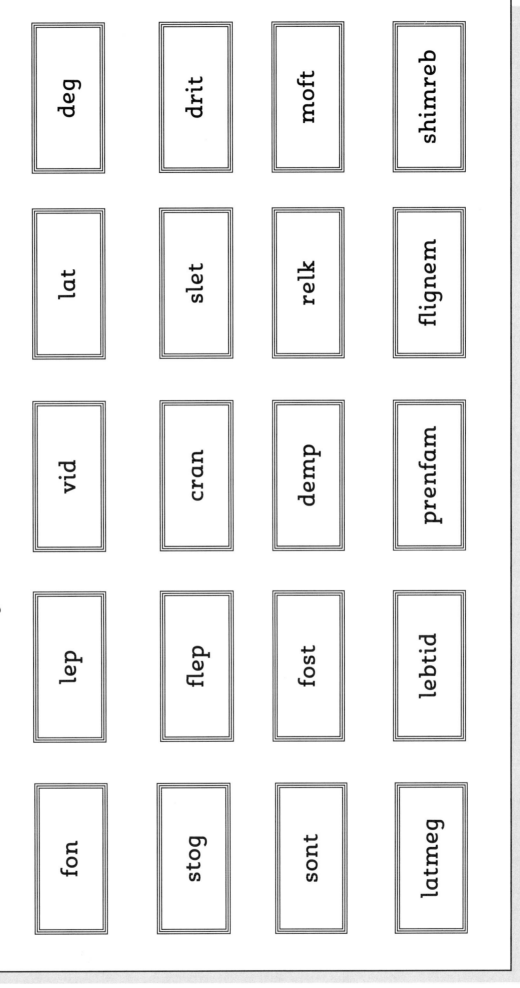

fon	lep	vid	lat	deg
stog	flep	cran	slet	drit
sont	fost	demp	relk	moft
latmeg	lebtid	prenfam	flignem	shimreb

Use the following sequence, adapted to the sounds with which the student has a problem.

> ## Voiced and voiceless phonemes
>
> Some phonemes use vibration of the vocal cords (e.g. /g/ /d/) and some do not (e.g. /sh/ /h/). There are some pairs of phonemes in which the only difference is the voicing or lack of it, e.g. /t/ /d/, /k/ /g/, /p/ /b/.

/t/ /d/ confusion

The following activities are for work on the possible /t/ /d/ confusion. This sequence of activities may be used for any pair of sounds which the student confuses.

1. Ask the student to make the voiceless phoneme /t/ and to feel the puff of air by holding a hand in front of the lips. Then ask the student to make the voiced phoneme /d/ and feel the vibration of the vocal cords by holding fingers against the neck. **Use this step only for voiced/voiceless pairs**. Otherwise start with Step 2.

2. Ask the student to listen for just one of the sounds, /t/, in a string of different phonemes and to clap and write the letter each time he hears it.

   e.g. /g/ /l/ /m/ **/t/** /v/ etc.

3. Ask the student to listen for both sounds, /t/ and /d/, in a string of sounds and put a token in the appropriate box labelled with the letter when the sound is heard.

   e.g. /m/ /l/ **/t/** /g/ /f/ **/d/** /r/ etc.

Cont'd

4. Now add a vowel **sound** to each consonant and ask the student to listen for the /t/.

   e.g. *me, he, she,* **t***ea, see, key* – then *my, low, more, far,* **t***oe*

5. Use the sound, /t/, at the end of a word and ask the student to listen for the /t/.

   e.g. *off, all, ou***t***, ace*

6. Finally use the sound, /t/, in the middle of a word and ask the student to listen for the /t/.

   e.g. *hello, inner, cushion, be***tt***er, having*

Repeat Steps 4, 5, and 6 with /d/. The whole sequence can be followed with other confused sounds.

The Edith Norrie Letter Case distinguishes between voiced and unvoiced phonemes by colour, making it a useful teaching tool for auditory discrimination.

Syllable Division

These words have syllables which can be heard clearly.

arithmetic	dragonfly	belonging	fisherman
boomerang	footballer	calendar	important
butterfly	invention	coconut	kingfisher
chimpanzee	discover	defending	multiply

supersonic rockets

wonderful and marvellous

addition and subtraction

kilometres and centimetres

magazine competition

television programme

butterflies and dragonflies

volcanoes and earthquakes

telephones and tape recorders

rectangles and triangles

outstanding targets

computer programmes

buttercups and blackcurrants

fantastic advertisement

Onsets and Rimes

When making activities and games for onset and rime, begin with simple onsets and rimes such as:

Onsets

b   d   f   h   j   l   m   n   p   r   s   t

v   y   z   sh   ch   th

Rimes

ag eg ig og ug   at et it ot ut

an en in on un   ab eb ib ob ub

ad ed id od ud   ap ep ip op up

am em im om um

Then add consonant blends and digraphs as onsets:

> **Digraph** – two letters making one sound, e.g. *sh*, *th*.

sp st sm sn sl cr gr fr bl cl

gl pr tr dr pl spr thr spl shr str scr

sh th ch

and rimes with consonant blends or digraphs:

ash esh ish osh ush   ast est ist ost ust

ang eng ing ong ung   ant ent int ont unt

amp emp imp omp ump   and end ind ond und

Non-words

These non-words are suitable for encoding and decoding activities and games. Start with the easier non-words in the first lines and progress to the later words, as students become proficient.

bip	tep	hap	sim	nop	gat
hin	feg	lup	reb	lon	cag
stip	frot	shem	clep	chid	tham
flet	grad	prot	swen	splut	shrom
spomp	grilk	prist	stong	strint	shramp
clunch	chank	flest	dingth	plont	spreng

bimlop	famlig	replat	ligsom
degfod	lodfim	gatyom	septeb
vempsolf	slidheng	flanghalp	breshpamp
slishlemp	swushtilp	benkslom	streplonch

Word Chains

twig ... twit ... twist ... twin ... win ... wins ... wink

sap ... slap ... slop ... slot ... lot ... lots ... loft ... soft

cap ... camp ... cramp ... clamp ... lamp ... limp ... lip ... lips ... slips ... slip
... trip ... strip ... rip

ham ... hum ... chum ... chums ... chump ... champ ... lamp ... lamps ...
limps ... limp ... lip

cop ... crop ... crops ... stops ... tops ... taps ... tap ... map ... maps ... mops
... mop ... hop ... shop ... ship ... hip ... hips ... tips ... tins ... tint ... tints ...
hints ... hunts ... shunts ... shunt

chat ... chats ... hats ... hits ... hit ... hint ... hunt ... hut ... hot ... shot ...
shop ... hop ... hog ... hogs ... hugs ... rugs ... shrugs ... shrug

clam ... cram ... crams ... cramps ... ramps ... ramp ... ram ... rim ... trim
... trims ... trams ... traps ... tramps ... tramp ... trump ... trumps

cot ... cost ... lost ... lot ... got ... get ... gut ... gust ... rust ... crust ... crusts
... rusts ... rust ... rut ... rat ... rant

Phoneme Deletion

These words are for phoneme deletion activities and games.

NB The student does not see the words. They are read to him.

- Ask the student to say the word with the first sound missing, e.g. *slate – late.*

- Sometimes a real word will be left; at other times it will be a non-word.

slate	cloak	plate	skate
place	sleep	cloud	bloom
flame	glide	smile	slide
sweet	throat	cream	spoon
snowed	groan	creep	fried
grass	style	float	crowd
crawl	frog	played	slope
drain	class	state	sleet

A harder game is to say the words with the first or the second or the last sound missing according to the throw of a die.

For numbers on the die,

- 1, 2 – say without first sound, e.g. *slate – late*

- 3, 4 – say without second sound, e.g. *slate – sate*

- 5, 6 – say without last sound, e.g. *slate – slay.*

Aim: to recognise syllables in a word.

Read the following sentences with a partner, saying one syllable each.

'The Flesh-lump-eat-er is long-ing dear-ly to guzz-le her up,' the BFG said smi-ling a litt-le now.

'We've absolutely *got* to stop them!' Sophie cried. 'Put me back in your pocket quick and we'll chase after them and warn everyone in England they're coming.'

'Redunculus and um-possible,' the BFG said. 'They is going two times as fast as me and they is finishing their guzzle before we is halfway.'

Taken from the *The BFG* by Roald Dahl

Aim: to recognise syllables in a word.

Say/write down 5 words with:

2 syllables

3 syllables

Say/write down 2 words with 4 syllables

Say/write down 1 word with 5 syllables

Aim: to recognise syllables.

Say/write a sentence with:

4 syllables

6 syllables

8 syllables

10 syllables

12 syllables

Aim: to improve rhyming.

Say/write down 5 words which rhyme with:

hill ...

cart ...

high ...

think ...

name ...

spend ...

Aim: to practise alliteration.

Make up phrases with words which all start with the same sound:

e.g. People polishing purple pies.

t ...

m ...

d ...

b ...

l ...

Aim: to work on taking away letters and sounds.

Take away a letter from each of these words to leave a new word:

e.g. spit – p = sit

Say both words aloud.

spent	lamps	sting	loft
drips	hunt	cramp	vest
pest	strap	swing	crash

Aim: to practise alliteration.

Say/write down 5 words which start with:

ch ...

sh ...

th ...

sp ...

st ...

cr ...

cl ...

gr ...

Aim: to practise alliteration.

Add an adjective to each name starting with the same sound:

e.g. Sunny Sam

Harry   Megan

Sophie   Kylie

Poppy   Rashid

Joseph   Dave

Andy   Zoe

Word Reading

The aims of reading at single word level should be:

- fluency
- automaticity, i.e. the word is read immediately
- speed
- comprehension.

Broadly speaking, there are three ways of reading a single word:

1 On sight

Skilled readers read most words 'on sight'. They look at the word on the page and immediately know both its meaning and its pronunciation. This allows them to read fluently and at speed, and to focus on comprehension skills such as the meaning of the whole sentence, inferences or the author's intention.

Consistent and automatic recognition of words at speed will improve comprehension at word, sentence, paragraph and text levels. Being able to read words on sight is therefore highly important to develop competent reading.

2 Decoding

New words may have to be decoded on several occasions before they become known 'sight' words. The reader needs to:

- know the sounds of the single letters and letter combinations
- know the letter names

- be able to see the similarity in letter patterns and hear the similarity in the sound patterns (rhyme)
- know about syllable division and morphology.

> **Morphology** = knowledge about morphemes.
>
> Morphemes are the units into which words can be broken to link with their meaning. These units are *prefixes, root words* and *suffixes. Prefixes* occur at the beginning of words and *suffixes* occur at the end. They change the meaning of the root word, e.g. *cook* is a root word, the meaning of which changes according to the addition of prefixes and suffixes such as *cooked, precooked, cooker, uncooked, cooking,* etc.

Decoding, including knowledge of letter names and sounds is introduced in Chapter 2 'Introduction to Decoding' and is fully discussed in Chapter 3 'Phonological Awareness and Phonics'.

Recognition of frequent letter strings and an immediate link with their pronunciation helps to speed up the decoding process. **Prefixes** and **suffixes** are therefore particularly important letter strings, not only because they occur frequently but also because they give clues to the meaning of words, e.g. *un* meaning *not* in *unread, unhappy,* etc.

Words which readers initially decode, should gradually become more familiar until they are read automatically on sight. Each time the reader sees the word the decoding process may be faster or consist of fewer steps. For instance, *Saturday* may initially be sounded out letter by letter and each letter sound blended in sequence to produce the full word, but later on the letter strings *Sat* and *day* may have become automatic and the word blended syllable by syllable. Finally, the word is read on sight with immediate knowledge of the pronunciation and meaning.

3 Context

If the word is in a phrase or a sentence, or there is an illustration accompanying the word, context can be helpful to guess what the word may be.

- **Grammatical structure** of the sentence will give clues to the part of speech:

  e.g. *Megan and her friend both smiled and started to ...*
  The missing word is likely to be a verb, such as *laugh* or *talk*.

  Marie-Louise was sitting between her two ...
  The missing word is likely to be a plural noun, such as *brothers* or *friends*.

- **Word knowledge** will give clues to the sort of meaning the word will have:

  e.g. *Joseph yawned, turned over in his comfortable ... and closed his eyes.*
  The missing word is likely to be *bed* or *cot*.

- **Pictures, illustrations** such as graphs or diagrams, titles and captions may also give clues to the unknown word.

Context on its own is an unreliable method of reading words but:

- it is a useful extra strategy for help when making a guess (e.g. the word might be *friends*, and it does start with *fr...*)

- it can be useful to check the sense when part of the word has been decoded (e.g. the letters *fr* have been sounded out and the context indicates that *friends* would make sense).

Different types of words

When learning to read new words (which are on their way to becoming sight words) different strategies may be more appropriate according to the type of word.

As described more fully in Chapter 3 – 'Phonological Awareness and Phonics', there are basically three types of words in English:

- **Absolutely regular**, e.g. *hut, stamp, mist*.
  These can be read by sounding out letter by letter, and blending the sounds together to say the whole word.

- **Words which follow phonic rules**, e.g. *came, light, hill, rabbit*.
  These can be read by a combination of sounding out the letters and by knowing, and applying, the phonic rules.

- **Irregular words**, e.g. *said, because, yacht*.
  Sounding out letters and knowing phonic rules helps a little with these words as there is some correlation between the letters and the sounds, e.g. **s**ai**d**, **because**, **y**a**cht**.

  However, as some letters are not related to the sound pattern, the reader has to place more emphasis on recognising the letter string as a whole.

How do words become sight words?

Readers need to be able to link the written word with its meaning as fast as possible. To do this they may use the following techniques:

- **The look of the word** including its overall shape, length and the exact sequence of letters.
  For instance, *good* has four letters, a tail at the beginning, two round *os* in the middle and a tall letter at the end. Note that attention to quite small differences in letter sequence is needed to distinguish *good* from *gold*.

- **Pronunciation of the letter/sound links.**
  This requires a knowledge of the most likely sounds for the letters, such as */k/* for *c*, as well as variations, such as */s/* for *c*. In English we have considerable variability in the links between sound chunks and letter chunks.

  > e.g. The sound */sh/* may be represented by *sh* as in *cushion*, *ch* as in *bunch*, *ti* as in *caution*, etc.

  > The letter *c* may be sounded */k/* as in *cat*, */s/* as in *city*, put together with *h* to sound */ch/* as in *church*, etc.

Knowing phonic patterns and rules will enable students to predict the likely pronunciation. For instance, understanding the silent *e* rule enables reading of unfamiliar words which also have *e* following a vowel and a consonant. Being able to read *late* may enable the reader to read *nape* if he understands the rule.

Some simple phonic rules apply to pronunciation. For instance, if a word has a double consonant, it is likely that the vowel sound in front of the double consonant is a short vowel.

> e.g. *hopping* as opposed to *hoping*.

Understanding of rhyme enables students to make analogies between words.

> e.g. being able to read *bank*, will facilitate reading *thank*, *sank*, *crank*, etc.

This extends to more than one syllable,

e.g. being able to read *advancing* will facilitate reading *dancing, prancing, lancing.*

Pronunciation of letter strings as a unit increases the speed of reading. These include frequently occurring letter strings such as prefixes, e.g. *re, un* and *pre*, suffixes, e.g. *tion* and *ing* and rimes, e.g. *and* in *band, sand* and *land.* These are especially important for easy reading of polysyllabic words, e.g. *im-port-ant, in-ter-jec-tion.*

Important groups of words for sight reading

High frequency words

In the early stages of reading a student who can read high frequency words on sight will gain fluency more rapidly. This is because a relatively small number of words comprises a large part of the word count for much text. Focus on these words with beginning readers or those who struggle to decode most words.

The McNally list of high frequency words, the Dolch Basic Sight Vocabulary and the National Literacy Strategy list are all useful sources of high frequency words.

See Sheets 4.1 and 4.2

See Sheet 4.1 – 'McNally High Frequency Words' and Sheet 4.2 – 'Dolch Basic Sight Vocabulary'.

Subject-specific vocabulary

For each subject or topic there is vocabulary which is specifically linked.

For instance, in learning History, it is necessary to know such words as:

year   reign   timeline   century   ancient

Within subject areas there are words which are specifically linked to topics. For instance, in learning about the Romans in History the vocabulary would be likely to include:

viaduct   atrium   baths   chariot   aqueduct

When students come to learn and study they need to be able to read these words on sight. Glossaries at the end of textbooks are a useful source for these words.

Words for life skills

All students need to be able to read instantly the words in their environment which give essential information. These include words on signs such as:

Ladies   Stop   Push   Gentlemen   Poison
Danger   Exit   No entry   Private   Way In

Many of these words are necessary for everyone. Indeed, some could make the difference between life and death. Necessary vocabulary will also vary according to the individual. For instance, vehicle drivers need to be able to read road signs quickly whilst they are driving.

Prefixes, root words and suffixes

Teach students the meanings of prefixes and suffixes so that they can use these to decode and understand new words.

The list of prefixes and suffixes on the following pages is taken from the Ladybird book, '*Spelling and Grammar*' compiled by Dorothy Paull.

Prefixes	Meanings	Examples
a	on, as, in	afloat, aboard
a, ab, abs	from, away	absent, averse
ante	before	antemeridiem (before noon or morning)
bi, bis	two or twice	biennial, bicycle
circum	around	circumspect, circumference
com	with, together	companion, communicate
contra	against	contradict, contrary
de	down	detract, deter, demote
dis, dif	not	distaste, differ
ex	out of	exit, exhale, expire
fore	before	foreword, forecast
im, in	into	import, include
in, im	not	impossible, immune, incapable
inter	between	interval, interrupt
mis	wrong	mistake, misapply
ob	against	obstruct, object
post	after	postpone, postwar
pre	before	prefix, preface, prepare
pro	for, forth	propose, profit, produce
re	back, again	repeat, remain, retake
sub	under	substandard, submarine, submerge
trans	across	transport, transfer, translate
un	not	unusual, uninhabited, undetected
vice	deputy, instead of	vice chairman, vice captain

Suffixes	Meanings	Examples
-able, -ible	capable	suitable, edible
-ain, -an	connected to	publican, chaplain
-ance, -ence, -ment, -ness	in a state of	repentance, existence, amusement, hopelessness
-ant, -er, -eer, -ier	someone who	servant, assistant, grocer, engineer
-ess	female form	lioness, princess
-fy	to make	magnify, purify
-less	without	timeless, fearless
-ling, -ock	little	duckling, bullock
-ory	a place for	factory
-ous	full of	monstrous, victorious

ASSESSMENT

Use appropriate lists of words to check students' ability to read on sight. Be careful to note whether there is a delay, even slight, in reading the word aloud. This means that some strategy, such as sounding the word out, is being used and that reading is not **fully** automatic.

 See Sheets 4.1 and 4.2

Use lists such as Sheet 4.1 – 'McNally High Frequency Words' and Sheet 4.2 – 'Dolch Basic Sight Vocabulary'.

Ask the student to read the words aloud as quickly and accurately as possible and note whether each word was read:

- correctly
- immediately.

Those, which are read after a delay will need further practice to become automatic.

Use lists of topic or subject words as appropriate to identify those words which need teaching in order that a student may read texts with ease.

David Wilson of Harton School's Equal Opportunities department has created a web portal providing access to a series of vocabulary lists and activities for use in teaching each of the National Curriculum core and foundation subjects: Art, Design Technology; English; Geography; History; Information and Communication Technology; Mathematics; Modern Foreign Languages; Music; Personal; Social and Health Education and Citizenship; Physical Education; Religious Education; and Science.

The School Subject Keywords home page is at
http://www.tomwilson.com/david/NC/Keywords/Index.html

Vocabulary activities to make the vocabulary more accessible to students with specific learning difficulties can be found at
http://www.tomwilson.com/david/NC/Keywords/Hartonkeywords.html

In order to assess a student's single word reading age in relation to other students of his age, standardised tests giving age norms are available, such as:

The Dyslexia Screening Test
The Psychological Corporation, 24–28 Oval Road, London NW1 7DX

WRAT 3 (Wide Range Achievement Test)
The Psychological Corporation, The Boulevard, Langford Lane, Kidlington, Oxford OX5 1GB, Tel: 01865 888188

NFER Graded Word Reading Test
NFER-NELSON Publishing Co Ltd, The Chiswick Centre, 414 Chiswick High Road, London W4 5TF Tel: 0845 6021937

NB. Whilst it is, of course, desirable to practise words in subject and topic lists which need to be learnt, words in standardised tests must not be taught as this would invalidate any subsequent test results.

Aim to build up students' ability to use both visual and sound based information about words, as well as encouraging them to use context as an additional support.

Go back to Chapter 3 'Phonological Awareness and Phonics' for full information on building the essential phonological awareness skills which underpin decoding.

Wherever possible, link the following activities to students' immediate needs. Use topic or subject-specific vocabulary and the vocabulary needed for their learning, tests and exams.

- **Ask students to find words which rhyme** and are spelt the same way at the end, such as *light/fight*.

- **Write topic words on cards** and place face down. Each student in turn picks up two cards and says a sentence with them both in.

  e.g. 'Max wanted to see the *frescoes* in the Italian *chapel*.'

- **Give the plastic letters (or letter cards) of a word in random order** and ask the student to put them together to spell the word correctly. Give a clue to the word.

  e.g. *c r e h a i c t t* for *architect*.
  Clue: someone who designs buildings.

  e.g. *u e s a q r* for *square*.
  Clue: a shape with four equal sides.

See Target Card 4.1

- **Ask the student to group words** according to rhyme or the same number of syllables. This draws attention to the sound structure of the words.

  e.g. 2 syllables: *oyster / cowrie / coral / scallop*
       1 syllable: *conch / clam / pearl / whelk*

- **Play Bingo with similar looking words** to encourage attention to the precise letters in the words. Choose words which the students have confused. Be careful to ask an accurate reader to be 'caller'. An extension of this game would be to ask students to find words which look alike and to make their own game.

  e.g. *lone   lonely   alone   love   lovely   loved
       leave   loner*

  See Sheet 4.3 – 'Bingo Lookalike Words'.

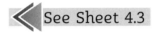
See Sheet 4.3

- **Write topic words on cards**. Draw attention to salient features such as letters with tails, double letters, tall letters etc. Ask the student to write a clue or draw a picture on the other side of the card for the meaning. Give these to the student to keep in a pocket and practise reading at intervals.

  e.g. *vegetation* – may have a picture of *vegetables* in the grass under the trees.

  e.g. *Capulet* – may have a picture of Juliet wearing a *cap*, and a note that her parents wouldn't *let* her see Romeo.

  Montague – may have the *M* highlighted, as there is also an *m* in Romeo.

- **Ask the student to highlight words within words.**

  e.g. **star** in cus**tar**d.

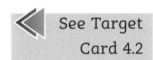
See Target Card 4.2

- **Give the student the letters of a polysyllabic word** in random order and ask for small words which can be made from the letters. Bonus points could be offered for spelling the whole word.

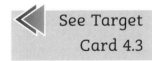
See Target Card 4.3

  e.g. *e a h c t c a r r*
       cat, chat, chart, etc. from the whole word *character*.

- **Ask the student to find a shorter word within a longer one** and to make up a silly sentence.

  e.g. cold: If you have a c*old*, you look *old*!
         think: If you *think* too much you might get *thin*!

See Sheet 4.4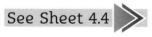

- **Write groups of single-syllable words which share rimes** on cards. Then ask the student to cut them all into onsets (the beginning consonants) and rimes (from the vowel onwards). Mix the cards up and then ask the student to put them together again in their groups and read.

- **Take topic words and ask students to determine the root words.** Then ask them to add prefixes and suffixes to make as many words as possible and to discuss their meanings.

  e.g. draw: *re*draw, *with*draw, draw*ing*, with*drawal*, etc.
         count: *re*count, count*ing*, count*ed*, *ac*count, *ac*count*able*, etc.

  Note that there will be some changes in spelling, e.g. *hope* + *ing* = *hoping* without the *e*.

See Sheet 4.5 ▷

- **Give a list of topic words and ask students to make a crossword** with clues including them all. Give squared paper. Then ask students to swap and do each other's crosswords.

  See Sheet 4.5 for a blank grid to photocopy.

See Sheet 4.6 ▷

- **Ask students to make a wordsearch** on squared paper with embedded words from their topic list. These should be 'hidden' horizontally only. They can then challenge a friend to find them.

e.g.
Find 'girl'
and 'boy'

b	j	g	i	r	l	m	o
b	o	y	u	w	s	a	q
d	f	r	n	i	r	z	c

- **Ask students to colour code the syllables in topic words.**

  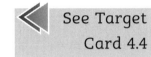
  See Target Card 4.4

  e.g. in *architecture, ar* = red, *chi* = green,
  tec = black and *ture* = blue.

- **Ask students to highlight prefixes and suffixes** in a list of topic words.

  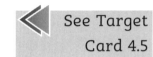
  See Target Card 4.5

  e.g. **dis**cord **un**fortunate**ly** **re**make
  unmention**ed**.

- **Write a long word chain without breaks between words** using words from a topic. Ask students to cut the card into words.

  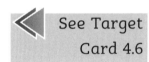
  See Target Card 4.6

  e.g. vegetablefloweringplantwoodenshootscuttingsoilannualbloom

- **Write a story or passage leaving gaps for the topic words.** Give these on cards and ask students to paste the words in the appropriate gaps.

  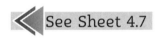
  See Sheet 4.7

  e.g.
  Harry was looking ... ... to next Saturday. His dad had promised to take him to the football ... ... at the local ... ... His closest ... ... , Tom, was going to come too. He really wished that ... ... and ... ... would pass a bit faster.

  match Friday friend Thursday forward stadium

- **Ask the student to organise topic words on cards into categories.** This will mean they have to read them accurately and also think carefully about the meaning. For instance, *centurion* could go into both

  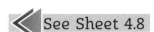
  See Sheet 4.8

People and **Army** categories in the following example from a topic on the Romans:

e.g.

People   Clothing   Army   Buildings

centurion   toga   temple   Colosseum   town house servant   stadium   senator   competitors   emperor armour   helmet   tunic   sandal   baths   general

- **Give the student a list of words to read and time him.** See if he can beat his own speed. Encourage regular practice. This would be a useful homework task.

See Sheet 4.9

- **Make a pack of cards with similar looking words.** Make two of each and ask your student to play these as Snap.

  e.g. *their   there   they   then   these   those*

- **For 'difficult' words, give the student Dingbat-type clues.**

  e.g. d   Look
       i
           a
             g
               o
   Shaky   n
                      a
                        l

  This is even more effective if the students come up with their own Dingbat clues. The energy they put into the creative process will help them to remember the letters.

- **Encourage students to create their own glossaries of topic words** for revision. If these are written on cards they can then be used as vocabulary lists, spelling aids and in projects; this will help students both to read and to recall them.

- **Give students some text and a list of topic words from the text**. Ask them to track from left to right, highlighting the words.

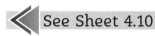 See Sheet 4.10

  e.g. Find: *rector   blazing   driven   figure   flames*
        window   Jack   awakened   alone   rafters
        groped   stairs   trapped

> The rector tried to fight his way back into the blazing house, but in vain. Again and again he was driven back. Then a small figure appeared against the glow of the flames at an upstairs window. Jacky Wesley had awakened to find himself alone in the house with the rafters above his head ablaze. He groped his way to the head of the stairs, only to find them in flames. He was trapped.

From: *John Wesley, Founder of Methodism –* published by Methodist Publishing House in agreement with Ladybird Books Ltd.

- **Give each student a list of consonants and consonant blends**.

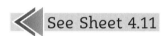 See Sheet 4.11

b	c	d	f	g	h	j	k	l	m	n
p	qu	r	s	t	v	w	y	z		
bl	br	cl	cr	dr	dw	fl	fr	gl	gr	pl
sc	sk	sl	sm	sn	sp	st	sw	tr	tw	scr
shr	sph	spl	squ	str	thr					

  Then give a number of rimes, or two-syllable words without the first onset, and ask them to make as many words as they can by adding a consonant or consonant blend to the beginning.

  e.g. Make as many words as possible by adding a consonant or consonant blend to the beginning of *...ash* (giving b*ash*, c*ash*, d*ash*, g*ash*, etc.) or *...ooking* (giving c*ooking*, l*ooking*, etc.).

- **Give students a sheet of words with a mixture of words which have either single or double consonants** between two syllables. Remind them

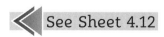 See Sheet 4.12

that the double consonant is likely to mean that the vowel in front has its short sound.

e.g. *bottle, stopping* – where the *o* is a short /ŏ/.

Tell them that when there is a single consonant between the syllables, they need to try both short and long vowel sounds to see 'which one sounds right'.

e.g. *robin* – where the *o* is a short /ŏ/
robot – where the *o* is a long /ō/

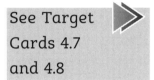

See Target Cards 4.7 and 4.8

- **Give students a prefix**, explain its meaning and ask for as many words beginning with it as they can make.

e.g. *tele* (meaning over a distance) to make *telescope, television, teletext,* etc.

Some common prefixes are:
a be de en ex mis in re to un ad dis pre

Some less common prefixes are:
tele ante co inter manu sub super multi hyper hypo circum contra intra hemi mega micro centi photo

Resources

Excellent materials for further practice with single word reading activities can be found in:

1 Joanne Carlisle, *Reasoning and Reading* Levels 1 and 2. Educators Publishing Service.
2 A. Steers, C. Z. Peck and L. Kahn, *Solving Language Difficulties*. Educators Publishing Service.
3 Kristin Johnson and Polly Bayrd, *Megawords*. Educators Publishing Service.
4 Gillian Aitken, *Spotlight on Suffixes*. Robinswood Press.
5 A. J. Hardwick, *Making Sense of the First 90 Sightwords*.

McNally High Frequency Words

These are grouped in order of frequency:

1   a and he I in is it of that the to was

2   all as at be but are for had have him his not on one said so they we with you

3   about an back been before big by call came can come could did do down first from get go has her here if into just like little look made make me more much must my no new now off only or our over other out right see she some their them then there this two up want well went who were what when where which will your old

4   after again always am ask another any away bad because best bird black blue boy bring day dog don't eat every fast father fell find five fly four found gave girl give going good got green hand head help home house how jump keep know last left let live long man many may men mother Mr. never next once open own play put ran read red room round run sat saw say school should would yes yet bus apple baby bag ball bed car cat children cow cup dinner doll door egg end farm fish fun hat hill horse jam letter milk money morning Mrs. name night nothing picture pig place rabbit road sea shop sister street sun table tea today top toy train water sit soon stop take tell than these thing think three time too tree under us very walk white why wish work woman

Dolch Basic Sight Vocabulary

a	is	said	some	six	made	pull	round
I	me	away	from	today	sleep	before	only
too	look	run	fly	take	then	goes	pick
to	can	with	but	four	seven	small	when
two	good	that	as	say	right	pity	gave
the	brown	going	under	or	why	could	every
in	funny	did	over	they	please	fall	which
see	be	who	stop	work	upon	think	our
into	put	like	out	long	once	far	want
and	not	come	his	there	together	found	think
up	little	had	make	about	us	read	better
blue	one	saw	your	just	tell	were	clean
she	black	no	have	walk	ate	best	been
yellow	my	after	help	ask	where	because	never
he	at	yes	call	sing	many	grow	those
go	all	an	here	must	warm	off	write
you	so	three	went	side	laugh	draw	first
we	by	this	cold	myself	live	bring	these
big	do	around	has	cut	now	got	both
red	are	was	give	let	buy	always	shall
jump	him	what	will	again	very	much	own
it	her	ten	came	new	cold	does	hurt
play	on	get	find	well	would	show	eight
down	green	if	don't	how	hot	any	wash
for	eat	soon	fast	keep	open	try	full
old	of	its	am	drink	light	kind	use
ride	ran	five	carry	know	wish	done	start
white	sit	their	them				

these	those	theme
them	they	that
there	this	then

crash	crush	branch
brush	brunch	lunch
crunch	brash	bunch

spring	sprang	strong
sprung	strung	shrank
string	shrink	shrunk

chin	chum	champ
chap	chip	chops
chop	chomp	chips

strap	scram	strip
scrap	strum	trap
scrub	scraps	trip

snip	snaps	snug
snag	smug	snap
snubs	snip	snub

nine	pine	line	fine	brine
stage	rage	wage	cage	page
fright	flight	might	slight	sight
blank	prank	frank	stank	shrank
stop	drop	flop	crop	slop
groom	bloom	broom	loom	gloom
grape	drape	gape	tape	cape
bring	cling	fling	sling	sting
drill	frill	spill	still	trill

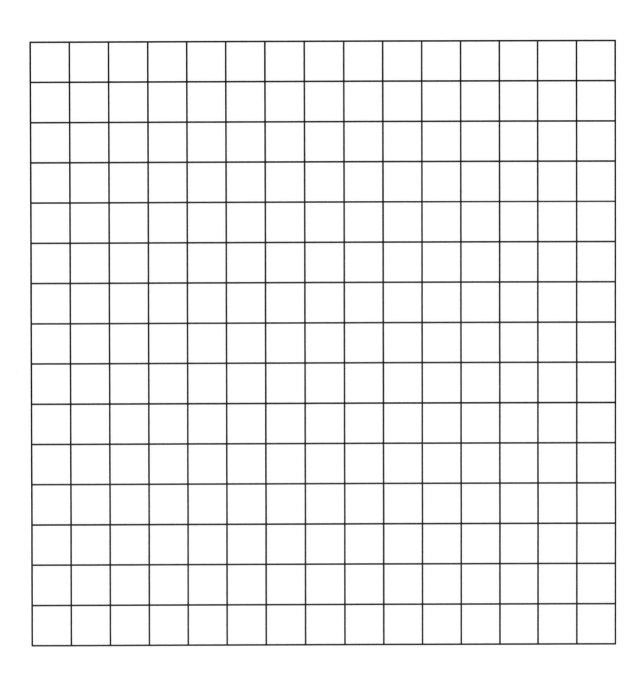

Word Search Grid

Use this grid to make a wordsearch. 'Hide' the words written below in the squares. You are only allowed to write the words from left to right.

Example

f	n	w	b	a	l	l	k	c	s	z	o	j	d	l
s	f	r	b	w	i	y	m	v	i	x	z	g	k	r

athletics   baseball   fencing   rugby   football   hockey   tennis
paragliding   cricket   skiing   sailing   rowing   tiddlywinks
darts   wrestling

Fill in the gaps with the topic words.

Topic words:

Jones   beer   snoring   Farm

bed

yard   drunk   night

lantern   boots

Animal Farm

Mr Jones, of the Manor ...., had locked the hen-houses for

the ...., but was too .... to remember to

shut the pop-holes. With the ring of light from his ....

dancing from side to side, he lurched across the ....,

kicking off his .... at the back door, drew himself a last

glass of .... from the barrel in the scullery, and made his

way up to ...., where Mrs .... was already

....

Taken from *Animal Farm* by George Orwell, published by Martin Secker & Warburg, 1945.

Categorisation

Find six words from the grid for each category. Tick them as you use
them.

Example

Numbers   seven, forty, hundred, eleven, fifty-two, thousand

Colours

Aircraft

Furniture

Sports

Feelings

Homes

tennis	red	glider	joy	navy	apartment
annoyance	chair	orange	cricket	fencing	house
cupboard	lilac	flat	athletics	wardrobe	sadness
purple	jet	anger	table	cottage	rugby
green	helicopter	bedsit	airship	football	seaplane
irritation	bomber	bungalow	misery	stool	desk

Snap

Make a pack of cards by photocopying each word five times onto card.
Cut into individual cards and shuffle. Play as Snap.

Game 1

from	for	four	frost	five
fame	fine	fun	first	fist

Game 2

these	their	there	they	then
thin	this	think	thank	them

Game 3

lost	last	list	lest	lose
love	live	lazy	lift	loft

Tracking

Look along each line of the passage from left to right. This is called tracking. Circle the words which are in the list as you go.

Robin ✓ salutes ✓ Nottingham pain cease pity mercy steal

families harry hunt castle blessed King North May

(Robin,) Lord of the Greenwood, (salutes) the Sheriff of Nottingham. We command you, on pain of death, to cease your cruel ways. Take pity on the poor, and have mercy on those driven to steal to feed their families. If you don't, we shall harry you night and day. We shall hunt you down, even in your own castle. This I swear, by God and his blessed Mother, and in the name of King Richard. Given at our Castle of the North Wind, in the merry month of May.

Taken from Chapter 3 of *Robin Hood* by Neil Philip, published by Dorling Kindersley, 1997

Making Words

Make as many words as you can by adding a consonant or consonant blend in front of the rimes which follow.

Example

b + ang = bang

Consonants and consonant blends

b	c	d	f	g	h	j	k	l	m	n	p

qu r s t v w y z

bl br cl cr dr dw fl fr gl gr pl sc

sk sl sm sn sp st sw tr tw scr shr

sph spl squ str thr

Rimes

ang ong ung ist oth ack

ace ice in all and en

Now make as many words as you can by adding a consonant or consonant blend to the beginning of these:

etting   ottle   ashing   anding   inging

Short/Long Vowels

- Read these words aloud.

- Remember if there is a double consonant the vowel in front of it will have its short sound, e.g. *flannel*, *kettle*, *pitted*, *bottle*, *suffix*.

- If there is one vowel between the two syllables, try both the long and short vowel sounds to see which one 'sounds right'.

- Mark the short vowels ˘ (**breve**) and the long vowels ¯ (**macron**)

robot	lemon	passage	linen	yellow
crocus	never	cabin	finish	later
habit	pupil	student	silent	rabbit
rubbish	recent	twitter	rival	robin
hoping	offend	hollow	cotton	shadow
stopper	hiding	rapid	happen	proper

4.2

Aim: to find short words within long ones.

Highlight a short word within each of the following words, e.g. **star** in **custard**.

pirate   discovery   occupy   friend   drink   cabin

crush   chime   glowing   aware   crusty   sparkling

piece   plaster   sticky   single   practical   holiday

4.1

Aim: to practise rhyming.

Find five words which rhyme and are spelt the same way at the end as each of these words, e.g.

fight: light, might, right, flight, bright.

bike:

keep:

stop:

book:

main:

4.4

Aim: to divide words into syllables.

Highlight each syllable in the following words in alternate colours, e.g. **department**.

coconut   skyscraper   opposite   intention

dinosaur   helpfully   reputation   obstinate

property   confident   magical   occupy

4.3

Aim: to make words from a string of letters.

How many words can you make using some of these letters? (You are allowed to use each one only once. You are not allowed to add any other letters.)

a   u   r   p   m   s   k   e   t   r

e.g. rap

Can you make one whole word from all the letters?

4.6

Aim: to recognise word boundaries.

Cut this string of letters into words, e.g.

orange/apple/tomato/grapefruit.

cucumbercarrotgreengageplumbananacabbage
orangeswedelycheepeachsquashpeaslimeapricot
raspberrylettucecressgooseberrypapayaturnippotat
o figmelontangerinedamsonbeanskumquatlemon
courgetteleekmushroom

4.8

Aim: to generate words using less common prefixes.

Make as many words as you can using these less common prefixes:

tele... anti... co... inter... manu... sub... super... multi... hyper... hypo... circum... contra... intra... hemi... mega... micro... centi... photo...

e.g. telescope, anticlimax, cooperate

4.5

Aim: to work on prefixes and suffixes.

Highlight the prefixes and suffixes of the following words in different colours, e.g. *unhelpful*.

Be careful! Some may not have both a prefix and a suffix.

unfriendly   importer   exporting   lately

blacken   darkness   represented   excitement

inhabited   outrageously

4.7

Aim: to generate words using common prefixes.

Make as many words as you can using these common prefixes:

a... be... de... en... ex... mis... in... re... to... un... ad... dis... pre...

e.g. avoid, become, depend

Visual Processing

Visual processing skills in reading include:

- **Visuo-spatial skills**, i.e. attention to:
  - position – where text is on the page
  - size – differentiating smaller and larger letters and words
  - detail – e.g. the dot on a lower case *i*, the cross on a lower case *t*, punctuation marks
  - shape – e.g. differentiating lower case *h/n*, *j/i*.

- **Visual memory**: the ability to recall letters and strings of letters, and the recognition of them when seen again.

- **Direction and eye tracking**:
  - word order – e.g. was she in the room? / she was in the room
  - letter/symbol order – e.g. *was/saw*, *form/from*, 67/76, 12/21
  - left/right scanning – starting at the left-hand margin and moving from left to right
  - up/down scanning – needed for lists, charts, mathematical problems, etc.
  - moving from one line of text to the next.

- **Reading words and symbols which are similar in shape to others** – which may involve any or all the above skills:
  - letters, e.g. *b/d/p/q*, *u/n*, *h/n*, *f/t*
  - words, e.g. was/saw, then/them, expect/except
  - numbers, e.g. 5/3/8, 6/9, 12/21
  - symbols, e.g. +/×, –/=

● **A variety of other visual skills** which are needed as automatic skills for fluent reading:

- focus – related to long/short sight, the need to move text further away from or closer to the eyes in order to be able to see it clearly. Fluent readers need to be able to shift focus quickly and easily
- binocular vision stability – the ability to use both eyes together to focus on text
- fusion – using both eyes at the same place at the same time, aligning the eyes and keeping them aligned when they are moving
- fixations – the eyes need to move smoothly from left to right and fixate on parts of the print. These movements are known as *saccades* and the pauses are called *fixations*
- field vision – how much can be recognised in one fixation.

ASSESSMENT

Use the checklist on Sheet 5.1 – 'Visual Processing'.

Include informal observation and assessment during the school day. Make a note of findings over a period of days in order to build up a picture of the student's visual processing.

See Sheet 5.1

Use Owen Leigh's Optometrist's checklist (see Sheet 5.2) in addition to the above in order to provide detailed information when referring for visual examination. Referrals can be made to:

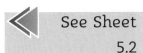See Sheet 5.2

- NHS Optician, and/or
- orthoptist or optometrist.

It is advisable to request an appointment with a specialist who is knowledgeable about reading difficulties and/or dyslexia.

When referring, ask for recommendations for the classroom to be given following the assessment. The student may also need glasses, eye exercises, coloured lenses or medical intervention.

ACTIVITIES

- **Give auditory and tactile support** when the student is dealing with visual information such as diagrams and flow charts, e.g. talk the student through the diagram as he points to the relevant parts.

- **Improve visual attention** by ensuring students focus on visual material before starting work on it.

- **Reduce amount of visual information**, e.g. cluttered pages with several diagrams, pictures, written text, etc.

75

- **Photocopy texts and add highlighting**, colouring or arrows to direct attention to salient points.

- **Choose reading books with care.** Barrington Stoke publishes fiction books which are 'reader friendly' for students with visual and other reading problems.

- **Follow the guidelines in Chapter 6 – 'Readability'** when designing worksheets or producing written texts.

- **Play 'Spot the Difference' games** with visually similar pictures (often found in comics and magazines).

- **Ask students to find Wally** in the *Where's Wally?* books by Martin Handford (Walker Books).

- **Encourage students to look at and read books which require visual noticing skills** to solve problems, such as *Turtle Quest* by Piers Harper (Walker Books).

See Target Cards 5.1–5.6

- **Ask students to sort and read similar looking letters or words**, e.g. *pdqb*, *these/them/they/there*. Make up cards to suit individual student needs.

See Sheet 5.3

- **Play Lookalike Bingo.** Make Lookalike Bingo boards to suit individual student needs.

- **Make, or encourage students to make, their own 'memory hooks'** to remember certain words,

  e.g.
  - a<u>r</u>e – say the letter in the middle.
  - could/would/should – write the common letters in colour and make a sentence such as 'Max **would** if he **could** and he **should** play football'.
  - two – has *two* dips in the letter <u>w</u>.

See Target Cards 5.7 and 5.8 See also Chapter 4, Sheet 4.10

- **Ask the student to scan for certain letters**, letter combinations or words. Use random letters or a photocopy of text from a book or magazine article.

### Writing and Drawing	
● Can the student copy from the board accurately?	
● Are drawing skills appropriate for age?	
● Are there many reversals of letters, numbers and words?	
● Are there problems with columns of figures in Maths?	
● Is hand/eye coordination adequate?	
● Is spelling over–reliant on 'sounding out', e.g. *sed* for *said*, *hoo* for *who*, *thay* for *they*?	
### Reading	
● Does the student recognise high frequency words consistently?	
● Does he close or cover up one eye when reading?	
● Does he move whole head when reading?	
● Does he tilt head at an odd angle when reading?	
● Can he read from the board?	
● Do his eyes 'jump around' the page?	
● Does he lose place on the page?	
● Does he hold the book too close?	
### Listen to the reader! Does he complain of:	
● Double vision?	
● Paper being too bright?	
● Blurry letters?	
● Letters jumping about?	
● Losing place on the page?	
● Headaches?	
● The print being too small?	

Optometrist's Checklist

This checklist of symptoms of visual problems observed at school and at home will help us understand how the child performs visually in his or her daily activities.

Please mark symptoms that occur frequently with two ticks, and occasionally with one tick.

Child's Name: ——————————————— Reported by: ———————————————

Reading
- Difficulty keeping place
- Skips or re-reads line
- Omits words
- Word by word reading
- Difficulty remembering reading
- Excessive head turning
- Tilts or turns head
- Poor sitting posture
- Holds head close to page
- Closes or covers one eye
- Rubs eyes during or after reading
- Short attention span
- Avoids reading
- Frowning, blinking, squinting
- Reverses words and letters

Writing and Other Desk Tasks
- Difficulty copying from the board
- Omits words or phrases
- Repeats words or phrases
- Confuses the order of letters
- Poor handwriting
- Difficulty staying on the line
- Writes neatly but slowly
- Immature pencil grip
- Poor finger movement when writing
- Draws with short sketchy lines
- Holds head too close
- Tilts or turns head to one side
- Restlessness while working at desk
- Not using other hand to support paper
- Squints or blinks looking up at the board
- Reverses letters or numbers

Body Posture and Space Awareness
- Unusual awkwardness
- Frequent tripping and stumbling
- Knocks thing off table/desk
- Difficulty with catching/throwing
- Confuses right and left directions

General Behaviour
- Avoids close work
- Distractible
- Unusual fatigue after close work
- Frequent signs of frustration
- Tension during close work
- Irritability or restlessness after visual concentration
- Headaches during/after school work

Appearance of Eyes
- Crossed or drifting eyes
- Watering or red eyes. When?
- Red rimmed, crusted or swollen lids
- Frequent styes
- Dark under the eyes

Questions for Children
- When does your vision go blurry?
- How can you make it clear?
- When do you see objects double?
- Do letters and lines run together?
- Do you have dizziness or feel sick when you use your eyes?

Owen Leigh BSc(Hons) MCOptom
Owen Leigh Optometry – The Vision Therapy Clinic, 28 The Spain, Petersfield, Hants GU32 3LA Tel: 01730 710174

Lookalike Bingo

Enlarge and photocopy each boxed group of words twice.

Cut up one set of words to be cards to match the Bingo boards.

● Each player has a Bingo board.

● One player is the caller.

● He shuffles the pack of cards.

● The caller reads out one card at a time.

● The player who has that word on his board claims the card.

● He covers the word on the board.

● The winner is the first one to cover his board completely.

strung	string	clunk
chunk	drink	stink
thin	chink	sting

thank	song	drunk
chin	sling	clink
bring	blink	blank

slung	drank	think
stung	clung	cling
clank	sprung	strong

Aim: to discriminate similar looking letters.

Cut up the letters in the box.
Sort them into groups which match exactly, i.e. they are the same letter.
Say the name of each letter.

p	d	q	b	d	g
b	g	p	d	q	b
p	b	d	q	g	q
b	d	q	b	d	q
p	q	g	q	b	p
d	q	d	b	p	b

Aim: to discriminate similar looking letters.

Cut up the letters in the box.
Sort them into groups which match exactly, i.e. they are the same letter.
Say the name of each letter.

h	n	m	w	v	u
n	m	v	m	n	h
h	u	n	h	w	m
v	h	n	v	u	u
m	u	u	u	v	w
w	n	w	m	n	h

Aim: to discriminate similar looking letters.

Cut up the letters in the box.
Sort them into groups which match exactly, i.e. they are the same letter.
Say the name of each letter.

i	I	t	f	j	i
t	I	f	i	i	f
I	t	j	I	i	t
f	j	i	f	j	i
t	f	i	i	t	f
j	i	f	I	I	t

Aim: to discriminate similar looking letters.

Cut up the letters in the box.
Sort them into groups which match exactly, i.e. they are the same letter.
Say the name of each letter.

w	v	x	z	s	w
z	x	s	w	z	z
s	w	v	x	z	w
v	z	s	s	w	x
s	x	z	v	s	v
x	w	z	w	v	s

Aim: to discriminate similar looking words.

Cut up the words in the box.
Sort them into groups which match exactly, i.e. they are the same.
Read the words aloud.

then	there	these	they	them	those
there	they	then	those	them	there
them	then	they	there	these	those
then	them	there	those	they	these
those	these	them	then	those	them
there	they	these	they	these	then

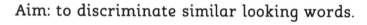

Aim: to discriminate similar looking words.

Cut up the words in the box.
Sort them into groups which match exactly, i.e. they are the same.
Read the words aloud.

thin	think	thank	thing	this	then
thing	thank	think	thank	this	thank
thin	think	then	thin	then	thin
then	thin	this	this	then	this
thing	thing	thank	think	thing	thing
thank	think	then	this	thin	think

Aim: **to improve eye tracking**.

Highlight every **e** in this passage.
Move your eyes from left to right along each line.
Start with the first line and move to the second and the third and so on.

fjems laqqe kklxze ftejavuj ez d geni oqnheks gfsei dfncea ilhs kl
bvskej qghels ebjhsu fdaio cbz ljaqide fh lg cke snla hj tsblai ogf
cnbv wlqjai jhbe skbwl hnd e kalsb nbsve ksi lsoep fkise hne balso
dklswe bsk hu nbskeh fbksoemns blsw pd hsknev plw dclsenb snbe
slp dvifnevkd alks ushend skldos nje sltrnois laoai pls nbe

5.8

Aim: **to improve eye tracking**.

Highlight every **ed** in this passage.
Move your eyes from left to right along each line.
Start with the first line and move to the second and the third and so on.

Next morning when the first light came into the sky and the sparrows
stirred in the trees, when the cows rattled their chains and the rooster
crowed and the early automobiles went whispering along the road, Wilbur
awoke and looked for Charlotte. He saw her up overhead in a corner near
the back of his pen. She was very quiet. Her eight legs were spread wide.
She seemed to have shrunk during the night. Next to her, attached to the
ceiling, Wilbur saw a curious object.

Taken from *Charlotte's Web* by E.B. White, published by Penguin Books.

Readability

Readability means that the reading level of written material matches the reading comprehension level of the reader.

There are formulae to work out these levels which use factors such as the length of words and the number of words in sentences. (See page 86)

Other factors to consider which are not so easily measurable, although they may be even more important are:

- content

- sentence complexity

- reader's attitude to the text, including motivation

- reader's previous knowledge

- language and concepts:
  - familiarity with the vocabulary
  - style and sentence structure
  - concrete versus abstract (some readers find concrete and visual language easier to understand)

- how well the text is organised; well-organised text can assist comprehension
  - headings
  - sub-headings
  - bullet points
  - sections or paragraphs

- kind of print:
  - font – type face
  - font size
  - spacing and justification
  - length of line
  - size of margins
  - colour of paper and contrast with the print (coloured print on coloured or 'busy' backgrounds can be especially difficult)

- illustrations used:
  - how many?
  - how big?
  - how detailed?
  - how close they are to the relevant information?
  - how much white space there is on the page?
  - how clearly diagrams are labelled?

- physical comfort
  - size of the book or text (some excellent readers will not read broadsheet newspapers because they are too big to manage!)
  - seating arrangements (these can affect the angle of the print which can be important for some readers)
  - adequate lighting (some readers find it difficult to read because they are sensitive to the flicker of fluorescent lighting – it is worth knowing that fluorescent lights can be modified to avoid this).

NB All these visual features of the text may matter less to good readers, but we know that many poor readers are affected by less than perfect visual processing. Refer to Chapter 5 – 'Visual Processing'.

Checking readability

Using a computer:

In Microsoft® Word you can display readability statistics, when you spell-check a document by ticking the appropriate box, in this order:

1. on the Tools menu, click options, and then click the Spelling & Grammar tab
2. select the Check Grammar with Spelling check box
3. Select the Show Readability statistics check box and then click OK.

When Word finishes checking spelling and grammar, it displays two scores which give information about the reading level of the document. They are:

- Flesch Reading Ease – this is scored out of 100, 100 being the easiest text; an average document is usually between 60 and 70
- Flesch–Kincaid Grade level – you need to add 5 to the score to come out with an English age equivalent.

Each readability score bases its rating on the average number of syllables per word and words per sentence.

Using the SMOG Readability Formula

This is quicker and easier to work out than any other readability formulae.

1. Select a text

2. Count 10 sentences

3. Count number of words which have three or more syllables

4 Mutiply this by 3

5 Circle the number closest to your answer

1	4	9	16	25	36	49	64	81	100	121	144	169

6 Find the square root of the number you circled

1	4	9	16	25	36	49	64	81	100	121	144	169
1	2	3	4	5	6	7	8	9	10	11	12	13

7 Add 8. This gives the readability level.

A readability level under about 10 will be understood by most people.

(From *Making Reading Easier*, The Basic Skills Agency, Admail 524, London WC1A 1BR)

Using cloze procedure

- Choose a piece of text between 100 and 150 words.
- Leave the first and last sentence intact.
- Delete every fifth word.
- Ask the pupils to fill in the missing words – spelling is not important!
- Accept any answer that makes sense and is readable.
- Percentage the scores.
- Anyone with 50% or more errors is struggling to make sense of the text.

Ways of helping the student read a new or difficult text are covered in detail in *Target Reading Comprehension*, *Chapter 6 – 'Listening to Reading'*. They include:

- **Discuss content** before you start reading, introducing any specialised vocabulary and possibly reading aloud some of the text.

- **Ask questions** to help direct the reading and small discussion groups to work out the answers.

Further activities

- **Choose high interest reading** materials when possible.

- **Check comprehension** of the text after reading.

See Target Card 6.1

- **Teach the 'five finger exercise'.** It is based on the statistic that text must be 95% readable in order for the reader to read unsupported and with understanding.

  - Tell the student to choose a piece of text about 100 words long. Give help, if necessary.
  - Ask him to read it and hold up one finger for each word that he does not know.
  - If he uses up all five fingers, the text will probably be too difficult for him.
  - If he uses up none it may be too easy.

  When he can carry out this method independently he has a strategy that he can use for choosing the correct level of book.

How to improve presentation of text and ease of visual processing

- Use at least 12 point font size.

- Use a sans serif font (like Arial without extra strokes).

- E x t e n d e d   s p a c i n g   c a n   h e l p (but don't make the spacing too wide).

- Condensed spacing is harder to read.

- DO NOT WRITE IN CAPITALS! IT IS DIFFICULT TO READ WORDS WHEN ALL THE LETTERS ARE THE SAME SIZE AND THE SHAPES OF THE WORDS BECOME SIMILAR RECTANGLES.

- Don't justify the line length. It is easier to read text when there is a ragged edge on the right-hand side and students are less likely to lose their place.

- Use grey, cream or pastel paper.

- Use dark grey rather than black print.

- Leave wide margins.

- Number bullet points.

- Box or highlight key words.

- Indent sections.

- Use clear simple headings.

- Leave lots of white space.

- Add pictures and diagrams, keeping them close to relevant text.

- Don't start a new sentence at the end of the line like in this example:
  Discuss the content of text before reading it. This will help your students ...

Making language more accessible in adapting texts and worksheets

- Use short sentences.

- Use simpler words; replace metaphors with literal phrases, e.g. not 'the proof of the pudding was that ...' but 'it was proved that ...'.

- Explain the meaning of complex words in brackets.

- Use active rather than passive, for example 'Complete the form' rather than 'The form should be completed'.

- Avoid abbreviations ('telephone' instead of 'tel') and acronyms ('European Union' instead of 'EU').

- Make it personal – use **you**.

- Avoid commas, brackets and link words, such as 'either ... or' constructions.

Designing worksheets

- Put key words in a box at the beginning and use as a word bank

- Box important information and instructions:
  - explain before work begins
  - use to help plan organisation of written work.

- Use clear simple headings:
  - have several headings on the page to break up text
  - underline or highlight/shade key words.

- Make the presentation interesting:
  - this is good for motivation
  - it also helps memory.

- Break up text with pictures and diagrams. This helps understanding.

- Use double spacing.

- Leave white space.

- Limit the number of instructions.

Resources

The A-Z of Reading Schemes reports on hundreds of reading schemes and is available in book or CD format from Nasen www.org.uk.

Individualised Reading Lists Key Stage 2 books are grouped according to National Curriculum levels. From the Reading and Language Centre, tel 0118 931 8820 www.ralic.rdg.ac.uk.

Aim: to check readability of a book or text.

- Choose a section of the text that is about 100 words long.

- Ask for help if you are not sure.

- Read the 100 words.

- As you read hold up one finger for each word you do not know.

- If you use up **all** 5 fingers the book is probably too difficult.

- If you do not use **any** fingers, it may be too easy!

- If you use 1, 2, 3 or 4 fingers, you will be able to read the text.

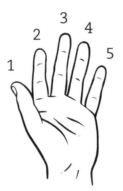

'If You Don't Know a Word ...'

This chapter covers ways to help readers develop strategies to tackle new words or words with which they are not familiar.

Use Sheet 7.1 – 'If You Don't Know a Word ...' to give to students to remind them of these strategies when you have taught them.

When a student has managed to read a word successfully for the first time, or you have told him what it is, encourage him to use a strategy to remember it. See Sheet 7.2 – 'Remembering a Word'.

When you are reading you will come across words which you don't know. Use these strategies to work the word out:

- Look at the letters carefully, say their sounds and blend them together, e.g. **f..r..o..s..t** to say **frost**.
  (Be careful not to add an 'uh' to any sounds, e.g. *fuh*.)

- Are there any groups of letters which are very common, that you can easily recognise?
  e.g. collec**tion**, wait**ing**.

- Is the word like another which you do know?
  e.g. **gu**ess might help you to read **gu**ilt.

- Can you divide the word into syllables and say each one and then blend them together?
  e.g. **dan..de..li..on** to say **dandelion**.

- Do you know another word which has the same ending? These might rhyme,
  e.g. knowing **knight** might help you to read **flight**.

- Read the sentence leaving out the word you don't know. Think what it might be.
  e.g. **The train pulled into the ... and stopped at the platform.**
  station is the likely word.

- Look at any pictures or diagrams. They might give you some clues.

- When you make a guess, check that the first sound is correct by checking the first letters of the word. Then check the end sound matches what you have said.

Remembering a Word

When you have first learnt a new word use one of these strategies to help you to remember it:

- **Flashcards 1**: Write the word on a card. Add a simple picture to help you remember what it is,
  e.g. cardiac – which means to do with the heart,
  so draw a heart.

- **Flashcards 2**: Write the word on a card. On the back of the card, write a sentence using it. If the next time you look at it, you have problems reading it, then write another sentence using it. Go on doing this until you have learnt it.

- Write the word in syllables, e.g. *spec..tac..u..lar.*
  Fold a piece of paper in half along its length (horizontally). Write the word on the underneath half. Then cut flaps in the top half to cover each syllable. Start at the beginning and practise saying the word in syllables as you lift each flap.

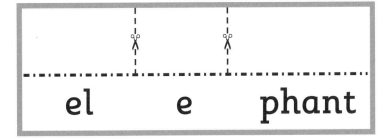

- Highlight the bit of the word which is difficult, such as 'silent' letters, e.g. **g**nome,
  or bits which are said in a different way, e.g. Wed**nes**day
  or letters or words which can be easily confused,
  e.g. **d**ull, **b**ull   **fir**st, **fi**st.

Cont'd

- Write the word with some others which rhyme and are written the same way,
  e.g. **flight**, **night**, **might**, **light**.

- Can you add any prefixes or suffixes to the word?
  e.g. **visit** could have a prefix: **re**visit
  or suffixes: visit**ing**, visit**ed**.

- Write the word in large letters on a card. Cut the word into letters and mix them up. Now remake the word and read it.

- If the word has an opposite, write both words on a card, e.g. *black* and *white*.

- If a word is one of a pair, write them together,
  e.g. *socks* and *shoes*.

- Keep any cards in your pocket and look at them often. A cheque cardholder is an excellent way of keeping them safe.

- If you keep getting stuck reading a word, do this:
  - write the word large on a sheet of paper or card
  - hold it up in front of you
  - look for any special bits, e.g. double letters, tall letters, letters with tails
  - pretend your mind is a digital camera and 'take a photograph' of the word. Any difficult bits could be bright colours to help you remember them
  - imagine the photograph on the wall
  - place the sheet of paper face down
  - now look up at the wall and imagine your photograph.

Reader's Toolkit

This final chapter gives suggestions for the teacher to discuss with a student. Students who understand their problems are more empowered to overcome them.

Read these bullet points with your student

- Reading is probably one of the most difficult things we have to learn to do when we come to school.

- Some students seem to learn this skill easily. For others, it seems a great struggle.

- Sometimes, when readers are struggling, their teachers give them more books, usually easier books and tell them to practise reading. If reading is hard, this may seem like a punishment rather than a help.

- Readers can learn to read more effectively if they have help to discuss where the real problem is and how to work it out. They can then work on small problem areas rather than the big skill of reading.

- We have a checklist to help us build up a reading toolkit just for you. This will help you to get better and better at reading.

 There are some questions on the checklist on the following pages for your student to think about and explanations for you to give them. Read it with your student and work out targets for reading practice together.

Checklist for **reader** to use with teacher support

Points for the reader to consider	Things to think about, things to do and targets to set for the reader	Action points for the teacher and suggestions for the reader
● Can I see the print clearly or is it blurred? ● Do I lose my place in the line of print or when moving to the next line? ● Do I have to use my finger to point at each word? ● Do I hold my book close to my eyes or have to screw my eyes up when reading?	If the answer is yes to **any** of the questions in this section, it might mean you need an eye check. If you cannot see very well, then you will find reading difficult. Don't worry, it does not mean you are going blind! Looking at words in books is a very different kind of eye activity to most of the looking we do in life. Talk to your teacher and get advice about the kind of vision specialist who would be best to check your eyes.	There is more information about this kind of problem in Chapter 5. Help your student to choose some Target Cards to work on from this chapter.
● Does my teacher say I leave little words out when I am reading or confuse small words?	If I leave little words out or confuse them, tracking exercises might help.	See exercises in Chapter 4 – Sheets 4.3, 4.9 and 4.10.
● I find it difficult to remember new words. The rest of the class see new words and remember them quickly. I think there is something wrong with my memory.	We all have different kinds of memory, e.g. you remember people's faces, what your house looks like, what time your favourite programme is on, etc. Memory for words and the order of letters in words is another kind of memory. For some it works easily. For others it takes a bit more practice, just like learning to ride a bike! Look out for written words at all times. They are all around you, on posters shop windows, notices on walls etc. Aim to become a good noticer of words.	Introduce your student to activities in Chapter 4. Together, you can decide on targets that he can work on, to help build this kind of memory. Work on easy, common words before you move on to difficult words that he does not see very often. Add Sheet 7.2 in Chapter 7 to his personal reader's toolkit to remind him of good ways to remember new words.

Cont'd

Points for the reader to consider	Things to think about, things to do and targets to set for the reader	Action points for the teacher and suggestions for the reader
	Even if you don't know what they are, you can sometimes guess what they say. Sometimes there are picture or symbol clues to help you guess. That's how you work out which toilet to use!	
• I find sounding out words very difficult. • I find long words difficult.	This could be because you find dealing with sounds difficult. Your brain deals with many sounds that your ears hear. Listening to music or cars go by is a very different activity from listening to sounds in words. Whole words can be much easier, especially if you understand what they mean. If you listen to *elephant*, you probably think of the animal rather than the combination of sounds *el-e-phant*. Teachers like you to sound words out because that helps you to work out words that you have never seen before. As you may have noticed, some words are easier to sound out than others.	It is best to check out your reader's skill with listening to sounds before you move on to looking at what the sounds look like when they are turned into letters. Chapter 3 is the best place to begin work on improving sounding out. Then you can add Sheet 7.1, Chapter 7 to his personal reader's toolkit to remind him of 'What to do if you don't know a word...'.
• I really don't enjoy reading. • The last thing I want to do is pick up a book. • The library is the last place I want to go to.	This is a shame because you have not yet discovered that books can be great and a really good way of passing the time. Maybe this is because you have not yet found a good book that will really absorb you and take you off to a different world, a bit like going to a really good film. Some people think reading is better than going to a film because you can make better pictures in your head.	

Cont'd

Points for the reader to consider	Things to think about, things to do and targets to set for the reader	Action points for the teacher and suggestions for the reader
• I really don't enjoy reading. • The last thing I want to do is pick up a book. • The library is the last place I want to go to	Good readers make good pictures in their heads. That is why you sometimes hear that people are disappointed when they go to a film of a book that they have read e.g. *Harry Potter* or *Lord of the Rings*, because the pictures in their heads were different ones! Never mind, there is plenty that we can suggest to help you like reading much more. Look at **non-fiction books** with good illustrations. Look at the **Internet**. Search for things you want to know about and you will find an enormous amount of information about anything you can think of. Many adults who have to read a lot for their work find this an easy way to get a lot of information. Maybe books are too hard or if they are easy they are too boring. If this is the case you might be able to work out whether you are reading the right level of book. You can do this with the five-finger exercise.	**Non-fiction books** – There are fewer words to read and there is a lot of information in the pictures and diagrams. Look at books about topics of high interest. Then your reader will have information in his mind already which will help him work out difficult bits. Another good thing about non-fiction is he can just read bits, and not have to start at the beginning and go right through to the end. The **Internet** is excellent for those who have had such a bad experience of books that they cannot bear to pick one up. Some kinds of software such as Text Help from IANSYST can read information to them. Finding the **right level** of reading is crucially important. Look at Chapter 6. Books may be too hard or, if easy enough, they may be too babyish. Look out for publishers

Cont'd

Points for the reader to consider	Things to think about, things to do and targets to set for the reader	Action points for the teacher and suggestions for the reader
• I really don't enjoy reading. • The last thing I want to do is pick up a book. • The library is the last place I want to go to		who sell books of high interest but low reading age. Discuss with your reader that writers can say things in a complicated way or more simply. *Many of us prefer the simple version, e.g. car instead of automobile.*
	You can find the right level with the five-finger exercise. Find a text of about 100 words and hold up one finger for each word you cannot read. If you hold up five fingers the text is too hard.	Teach the **five-finger exercise** from Chapter 6 and add the corresponding target card to his toolkit, if that is appropriate. *Look at ways of reading from Chapter 6 in Target Reading Comprehension.*
	Other things to try are **visualisation**, that is, making pictures in your head as you read, and **listening to stories on tape** which will help you increase your vocabulary. Books have many more words in them than you will hear talking to your friends or watching soap operas on TV. Once you find the right kind of reading it becomes a pleasant activity and a whole new world is open to you. Notice people on trains, buses and planes with their noses stuck into books. There must be a good reason for this!	*Chapter 9 in TRC gives practice in visualisation. Use Sheets 9.1, 9.2 and 9.3 for building this skill.* Guide the student to interesting stories on tape/CD. Find videos of texts he is studying.

Points for the reader to consider	Things to think about, things to do and targets to set for the reader	Action points for the teacher and suggestions for the reader
● I can read OK but I don't really understand it very well.	Good, you have made an excellent start to reading. You can turn the print on the page into the words that they say. Now onto the next stage which is building up understanding. You need to think about exactly where understanding is difficult to find where to begin.	Guide your student through the following comments in the next section 'Why understanding is difficult'.
Why understanding is difficult		
● I do not understand many of the words.	Sometimes writers use difficult words, e.g. *congenial* instead of *good fun*, *vocabulary* instead of *words*. Make sure the level of book is right for you. You may need to build up your vocabulary. Also, you can learn good ways of guessing what a word means from other clues in the sentence or the page. Good readers often guess and use clues to work out new words.	Check that he has the right level of text. See Chapter 6. *For vocabulary extension begin with activities in Chapter 3 – TRC. Guessing from context is an activity in Chapter 4 – TRC. See Sheet 4.1 – 'Words in Context' and you might suggest Target Card 4.1.*
● I understand the words as I go along but by the time I get to the end of the sentence I am not sure what it all means.	Sometimes sentences are too long or the words are in a difficult order. Working through different kinds of sentences will make you familiar with how to sort out what the writer means.	*There is useful help for this in Chapter 4 in TRC. Look at Target Cards 4.2, 4.3 and 4.4. Maybe, start with one and build up, when ready.*

Cont'd

Points for the reader to consider	Things to think about, things to do and targets to set for the reader	Action points for the teacher and suggestions for the reader
• I can answer the questions when the information is on the page, but sometimes the questions ask me what I think about something. I don't do as well with those questions.	That's well worked out and means that you realise there are different kinds of questions. Ones where the answers are easy to find on the page are what we call **literal questions**. Others are called **inferential questions** or **evaluative questions** where you have to work out something in your head.	*Work through the section on Inferences in Chapter 5 – TRC.*
	You may need help understanding phrases when they don't mean exactly what they say, e.g. *'He was down in the mouth'*.	*Explain and work through Chapter 4 – TRC to help with figurative language.*
• I read OK but I am very slow. • Sometimes I am so slow I have forgotten the beginning of the sentence by the time I get to the end!	Sometimes we get too used to reading word by word because that is how we started to read. Pointing at every word might slow you down. It is probably time to move on to the next stage. **Phrase Reading** is a good way to begin. Learning different strategies for different types of reading helps us to understand that we do not always have to read word by word. Learn how to **skim** (get your eyes working more quickly) and **scan** (find one piece of information on a page or in a book). These are the kinds of reading to use if you want to look in the paper to see when your favourite TV programme is on.	*See 'Phrase Reading' in Chapter 4 of TRC.* *See Chapter 7 of TRC 'Types of Reading' to learn how to skim and scan (find one piece of information on a page or in a book).*

Cont'd

Points for the reader to consider	Things to think about, things to do and targets to set for the reader	Action points for the teacher and suggestions for the reader
• I read quickly and sometimes so quickly I miss little details. Sometimes I misread important details in tests or Maths problems or homework instructions.	Reading for detail is another type of reading. This is the kind of reading you need to use when every detail matters, for instance the time the plane or train takes off: **18.30** is not the same as **8.30**; **3.30 a.m.** is not the same as **3.30 p.m.** Finger pointing might suit this kind of reading. It is important to learn <u>how</u> and <u>when</u> to **read accurately**.	*Chapter 7 in TRC has a section on* **accurate reading**; *this will help him to learn how and when to read accurately.*
• I am OK if the piece of writing is short but I begin to get lost and not understand with longer pieces.	This is normal. Sometimes we move too quickly to reading that is too long or complicated. We need to learn some skills to deal with longer pieces of writing.	*Chapter 5 in TRC gives you ways of helping your students understand longer texts.*
• My reading seems OK when I am doing it but I don't seem to remember much by the end.	Sometimes not much sticks in our heads when we read because we don't think enough about **what** we read. Then reading is an eye exercise. Our eyes move across the page, but we have not switched on the thinking part of the brain or it switches off as we get distracted. You need ways to get your brain into a higher gear.	*Chapter 8 in TRC will encourage your reader to be less passive in reading and capable of getting more out of the text.* *He may also need more practice with visualisation (see Chapter 9 in TRC).*
• If I have a project to prepare or a lot of writing to do, I do not know where to begin.	**SQ3R** is one way of studying what you read so that you understand better **while** you read and you recall what you have read more easily **afterwards.** You might review some other targets that you have been using such as **KWL.** If you have got as far as this in this checklist you are reading at a very advanced stage. Keep up the practice. People who read become better readers! Good luck!	At this stage he is ready to use more advanced strategies that bring together a lot of the work in TRC. Use **SQ3R** in Chapter 8. Sheet 8.13 – 'Dealing with Longer Texts or Books'. Sheet 10.1, page 177 gives steps to work through, **before** you read, **while** you are reading and **after** you have finished reading.

Answers to Exercises

Chapter 4

Sheet 4.12, page 70

Short vowel in front of double consonant:

hollow	passage	twitter	cotton	rabbit
rubbish	yellow	offend	happen	stopper

Short vowel with one consonant between syllables:

robin	proper	lemon	finish	linen
habit	rapid	shadow	never	cabin

Long vowel with one consonant between syllables:

rating	rival	later	hoping	pupil
silent	robot	crocus	recent	student

Target card 4.3, page 71

Whole word = supermarket

Glossary

Absolutely regular words are those where there is a distinct link between letters and sounds, e.g. stamp, act, frost.

Alliteration – words which start with the same sound, e.g. *house*, *Harry*, *home*.

Note that this does not always correspond with the same letters, e.g. *car*, *choir*, *kind*.

Automaticity – when a skill becomes spontaneous and effortless.

Bottom-up starts with learning about letter/sound links and using phonics. This is the approach used in *Target Reading Accuracy*.

Minimal pairs are pairs of words in which the difference in meaning is signalled by one sound only.

Morphology = knowledge about morphemes.

Morphemes are the units into which words can be broken to link with their meaning. These units are *prefixes*, *root words* and *suffixes*. *Prefixes* occur at the beginning of words and *suffixes* occur at the end. They change the meaning of the root word:

e.g. *cook* is a root word, the meaning of which changes according to the addition of prefixes and suffixes such as *cooked*, *precooked*, *cooker*, *uncooked*, *cooking*, etc.

Onset – the initial consonant(s) in a word or syllable.

Phoneme – the smallest unit of sound in a word.

Rule-based words are where a convention applies to a number of words, e.g. dropping the silent *e* before an *ing* ending, e.g. *hope* + *ing* = *hoping*.

Rime – the vowel and any letters after it in a syllable.

schwa vowel = an /uh/ sound.

Top-down uses knowledge of grammar and meaning to help predict words. This is the approach used in *Target Reading Comprehension*.

Recommended Reading and Resources

Turner, M. (1995) 'Children learn to read by being taught', in Owen, P. and Pumfrey, P.D. (eds) *Children Learning to Read*, Vol. 1. London: Falmer Press.

www.standards.dfes.gov.uk/literacy/publications
The Framework introduces the new term 'searchlights'. These are described as the different strategies which, it is explained, 'teachers know that pupils use to become successful readers'. They are given as: phonics (sound and spelling), word recognition and graphic knowledge (letter knowledge), grammatical knowledge, knowledge of context.
Fisher, R. (1995) *Teaching Children to Learn*. Stanley Thornes (Publishers) Ltd., Cheltenham.

John Wesley, Founder of Methodism, published by Methodist Publishing House in agreement with Ladybird Books Ltd

Joanne Carlisle, *Reasoning and Reading* Levels 1 and 2. Educators Publishing Service.

A. Steers, C. Z. Peck and L. Kahn, *Solving Language Difficulties*. Educators Publishing Service.

George Orwell (1945), *Animal Farm*. Martin Secker & Warburg.

Neil Philip (1997) *Robin Hood* (Chapter 3). Dorling Kindersley.

E.B. White, *Charlotte's Web*. Penguin Books.

Making Reading Easier. The Basic Skills Agency, Admail 524, London WC1A 1BR

Patricia Pothecary and Declan McCarthy, *Special Support Assistants: A Manual for School*. ISBN 0 9528526 0 8.

Phonological awareness assessments

Helen Arkell Dyslexia Centre Auditory Tests – Revised Version 2000
Helen Arkell Dyslexia Centre, Frensham, Farnham, Surrey GU10 3BW, Tel: 01252 797511

Phonological Assessment Battery (PhAB) by Norah Frederickson, Uta Frith and Rea Reason
NFER-NELSON Publishing Co Ltd, The Chiswick Centre, 414 Chiswick High Road, London W4 5TF,
Tel: 0845 6021937

Sound Linkage by Peter Hatcher
Whurr Publishers, Turpin Distribution Services Ltd, Blackhorse Road, Letchworth, Hertfordshire SG6 1HN,
Tel: 01462 672555

The Edith Norrie Letter Case is obtainable from the Helen Arkell Dyslexia Centre, Frensham, Farnham, Surrey GU10 3BW, Tel: 01252 79 7511

David Wilson of Harton School's Equal Opportunities department has created a web portal providing access to a series of vocabulary lists and activities for use in teaching each of the National Curriculum core and foundation subjects: Art, Design Technology; English; Geography; History; Information and Communication Technology; Mathematics; Modern Foreign Languages; Music; Personal; Social and Health Education and Citizenship; Physical Education; Religious Education; and Science.

The School Subject Keywords home page is at
http://www.tomwilson.com/david/NC/Keywords/Index.html

Vocabulary activities to make the vocabulary more accessible to students with specific learning difficulties can be found at
http://www.tomwilson.com/david/NC/Keywords/Hartonkeywords.html

In order to assess a student's single word reading age in relation to other students of his age, standardised tests giving age norms are available, such as:

The Dyslexia Screening Test
The Psychological Corporation, 24–28 Oval Road, London NW1 7DX

WRAT 3 (Wide Range Achievement Test)
The Psychological Corporation, The Boulevard, Langford Lane, Kidlington, Oxford OX5 1GB,
Tel: 01865 888188

NFER Graded Word Reading Test
NFER-NELSON Publishing Co Ltd, The Chiswick Centre, 414 Chiswick High Road, London W4 5TF
Tel: 0845 6021937

The A-Z of Reading Schemes reports on hundreds of reading schemes and is available in book or CD format from Nasen www.org.uk.

Individualised Reading Lists Key Stage 2 books are grouped according to National Curriculum levels. From the Reading and Language Centre, tel 0118 931 8820 www.ralic.rdg.ac.uk.

Appendix I

Normal development of reading

Many think that this is the way that children develop towards fluent reading of words:

They move through phases from **logographic** to **alphabetic** to **orthographic**.

1 **Logographic** phase is the earliest stage when:
   - children guess words based on a few obvious visual features such as a curvy 'm' for mcDonalds
   - they recognise their own written names
   - letter/sound links are not part of their reading knowledge
   - they cannot read new words without being told what they are.

2 **Alphabetic** phase begins to develop when:
   - children learn that letters and letter combinations are linked to sounds.

3 **Orthographic** phase is reached as:
   - children become familiar with groups of letters, such as *tion* and *ology*
   - words are recognised instantly
   - letter/sound combinations are used when words are unfamiliar.

These phases are not mutually exclusive. Children may have pockets of knowledge in areas of interest or expertise. They will be more likely to recognise:

frequently used words, absolutely regular words (where the word can be sounded out letter by letter) and rule-based words (where a convention applies to a number of words, such as dropping the silent e in *hope + ing = hoping*). They will find it harder to recognise less frequently used and irregular words such as *pneumonia, beauty, colonel*, etc.

Absolutely regular words are those where there is a distinct link between letters and sounds, e.g. stamp, act, frost.

Rule-based words are where a convention applies to a number of words, e.g. dropping the silent *e* before an *ing* ending, e.g. *hope + ing = hoping*.

As readers build up a 'bank' of easily recognised words they can begin to use other prompts, clues or 'cues' in reading.

The **3-cue system** in reading, now called '**Searchlights**' in the National Literacy Strategy, refers to the following cues:

1 **Grapho-phonic cues** – letter/sound links: words which are recognised from the letters on the page and are worked out phonically or read instantly at sight.

2 **Grammar cues** – the knowledge about the structure or order of words in sentences helps readers to predict less familiar words, e.g. *The two child ... were playing with their toys*.

A good knowledge of language and grammar will enable the early or developing reader to predict that more than one *child* will be *children* even if it is a word not read before.

3 **Meaning cues** – the early or developing reader who has a good understanding of word meanings and who has access to a good vocabulary will bring these skills to read new words, e.g. *They spent a f... on ice-cream.*

The reader with a good vocabulary may easily predict from the context that the word beginning with *f* is *fortune*; the reader who guesses *fiver* is similarly making a good guess from the overall meaning!

Good readers will access **all** cues as appropriate.

Appendix II

Reading tests

What reading tests tell you and what they don't:

There are many kinds of reading tests on the market. They range from:

- single word reading
- sentence reading
- prose reading.

They test:

- accuracy
- comprehension
- speed.

Consider these points when choosing how to test and what test to use:

- Some tests require readers to read aloud. That will give an accuracy score.

- If the reader reads silently only a comprehension score can be worked out.

- If a comprehension score is based on written answers to questions, the poor writer may not do himself justice even when he has understood well.

- If comprehension questions are asked after the reader has read aloud, he may not do as well as if he read silently. For some readers, reading aloud involves much more effort and creates high levels of stress.

In addition to the types of reading test described above, there are some tests which assess the ability to read **non-words**. These are designed to assess decoding of non-words which are either absolutely regular or rule based, such as **fleng**, and **boping**. These tests therefore assess decoding ability without allowing the reader to use the ability to read a word at sight. See the Helen Arkell Auditory Tests, Revised Version 2000, obtainable from the Helen Arkell Dyslexia Centre, Frensham, Farnham, Surrey GU10 3BW Tel: 01252 797511.

Single word or prose reading?

Ideally use both.

Single word tests measure:

- **sight vocabulary** – those words that a reader knows automatically
- **word attack skills** – the strategies that a reader uses when he meets an unfamiliar word without any contextual clues to help.

Single word tests therefore tap the first two searchlights in The National Literacy Strategy, **phonics** (sound and spelling), **word recognition and graphic knowledge** (of letters and letter combinations).

Prose reading tests provide a measure of all four searchlights:

- grammatical knowledge
- knowledge of context
- phonics
- word recognition and graphic knowledge.

Interpreting results

Treat scores with caution!

- Results are reported as Reading Ages and sometimes as Standard Scores.

- A Standard Score can range from 85 Low Average to 115 High Average with 100 being Average.

- Results of reading tests can confuse and mislead, as reading tests do not always compare well with each other.

- Developing readers do not necessarily increase their reading ability in tandem with their chronological age. Maturity may come in fits and starts.

- Two readers can achieve identical scores but have very different reading skills and strategies. When reading prose, one reader may make many visual mistakes, omitting or substituting little words, such as *of, for, from,* etc. This may still allow him to derive meaning as he reads the longer, content words accurately. Another reader may score similarly but make mistakes with longer words which affect the amount of meaning he is able to get from the text.

- Poor readers tend to fall into one of three categories:
  - poor decoders, where comprehension might be better but can only be as good as the decoding will allow it to be.
  - poor decoders and poor comprehenders.
  - good decoders, but poor comprehenders, sometimes known as hyperlexic readers.

Some guidelines for interpreting scores

Compare single word reading with prose reading.

- If prose reading is significantly better than single word reading, consider whether the reader is over-reliant on meaning and grammar to help his reading and look at activities in this book to bolster his skills at word reading.

- The same is true if in a prose reading test the comprehension score exceeds the accuracy score.

- If the accuracy score is better than the comprehension score on a prose reading test, the reader will benefit from the approach used in *Target Reading Comprehension*.

- Consider understanding of spoken language if reading comprehension is lower than reading accuracy. Comprehension may be poor for **spoken** language, in which case it cannot be expected in reading.

- If single word reading is significantly better than prose reading, consider whether the reader has visual tracking problems. See Chapter 5 – 'Visual Processing'.

Index

Acknowlegements

The publishers would like to thank the following for permission to use their copyright material. It is the belief of both the publishers and the authors that every effort has been made to trace copyright holders. However, should there be any omissions in this respect, we apologise and on receipt of relevant information, agree to make the appropriate acknowledgements in future editions.

ROALD DAHL: from *The BFG* Copyright © Jonathan Cape Ltd & Penguin Books Ltd, from *Revolting Rhymes* Copyright © Jonathan Cape Ltd & Penguin Books Ltd; from *The Ladybird Book of Spelling and Grammar*, compiled by Dorothy Paull, Copyright © Ladybird Books Ltd. 1984, from *John Wesley, Founder of Methodism* by permission of the Methodist Publishing House in agreement with Ladybird Books Ltd.; GEORGE ORWELL: from *Animal Farm* Copyright © George Orwell 1945 by permission of Bill Hamilton as the literary executor of the Estate of the Late Sonia Brownell Orwell and Secker and Warburg Ltd; NEIL PHILIP: from *Robin Hood*, Text copyright © Neil Philip, Copyright © Dorling Kindersley 1997; OWEN LEIGH: The Optometrist's Checklist Copyright © The Vision Therapy Clinic, Petersfield, Hants; E B WHITE: from *Charlotte's Web*, Hamish Hamilton 1952, Copyright © 1952 by J White; SMOG Readability Formula from *Making Reading Easier* published by The Basic Skills Agency, Admail 524, London WC1A 1BR.

Other titles in the Target Series:

Listening and Understanding in Secondary Schools
Meriel Davenport and Philippa Hall
ISBN 1-84299-157-4

Listening and Understanding in Primary Schools
Jeanne Reilly and Sarah Murray
ISBN 1-84299-158-2

Reading – Comprehension
Bernadette McLean and Rosie Wood
ISBN 1-84299-161-2

Self-esteem
Jenny Foster
ISBN 1-84299-159-0

Motor and Perceptual Skills
Louise Williams
ISBN 1-84299-160-4

You can order these books direct from:

Macmillan Distribution Ltd,
Brunel Road, Houndmills, Basingstoke, Hampshire RG21 6XS

Tel 01256 302699

Email mdl@macmillan.co.uk